**DO
SHA
PLAYS**

GW00373835

Selected Poems
?

From

'All's Well That Ends Well'
to
'Twelfth Night'

Compiled by

FRANCIS COOKE

POCKET REFERENCE BOOKS

Published by:
Pocket Reference Books Publishing Ltd.
Premier House
Hinton Road
Bournemouth
Dorset BH1 2EF

First Published 1996

Typesetting	Gary Tomlinson
	PrintRelate (Bournemouth, Dorset)
	(01202) 897659
Cover Design	Van Renselar Bonney Design Associates
	West Wickham, Kent BR4 9QH
Printing and Binding:	RPM Reprographics
	Units 2-3 Spur Road
	Quarry Lane, Chichester
	West Sussex PO19 2PR
	Tel. 01243 787077
	Fax. 01243 780012
	Modem 01243 536482
	E-Mail: rpm@argonet.co.uk

ISBN 1 899437 40 1

Contents   **Pages**

INTRODUCTION

Where did William Shakespeare's genius come from?

We know of the basic details of his background, but nothing can account for the astonishing greatness of his mind.

His father, John Shakespeare, was a glover and wool-dealer, owning his own business in Stratford. He had been apprenticed to a 'whittawer' (a white leather maker); had married Mary Arden, daughter of a gentleman farmer; and then had become bailiff (mayor) of Stratford and a Justice of the Peace at the relatively young age of 38.

However a few years later his wool business failed and at times John Shakespeare dared not leave his house for fear of being arrested for debt. His wife's inheritance had to be mortgaged to save him.

This, then, is William Shakespeare's family background. He was one of eight children, four boys and four girls: the third child and eldest son. Clearly he enjoyed a close family life.

William must have been 'one of the lads'. He was 18 when he made his future wife, Anne Hathaway, pregnant (she was 8 years his senior). They married and their first child, Susanna, was baptised five months later. Twins, Hamnet and Judith, soon followed, but these were their only children, and details of this early part of Will's life are virtually non-existent.

It is not until 1592 that we have any clear idea of Shakespeare as a person. Having met some travelling actors he had decided to try his fortune in London. Success followed success; he became a popular playwright and part-owner of a newly-built theatre; amassed comfortable wealth; and as a result he was able to rescue his father from debt. Old John Shakespeare was even able to obtain a coat of arms in 1596 and die a gentleman.

William Shakespeare had rescued the family fortunes, and in doing so he had produced a succession of some of the world's greatest literary works. Somehow, he had transformed his early reading and experiences into plays of extraordinary beauty, complexity and power.

Shakespeare's creative genius lasted for 25 years. And when he decided to retire to his home at Stratford he defined himself, in his lengthy will, as 'William Shakespeare, of Stratford upon Avon in the County of Warwick, gentleman, in perfect health and memory.'

Fittingly for one of the greatest of all English gentlemen, he died on St. George's Day, 1616, the national day of England, and traditionally his own birthday.

DAVID HILLIAM

WHAT DO <u>YOU</u> KNOW ABOUT SHAKESPEARE'S PLAYS? TRY THESE TEASERS

In which plays would you find the following quotations?

'I know a bank whereon the wild thyme blows,
Where oxlips and the nodding violet grows,
Quite over-canopied with luscious woodbine,
With sweet muskroses, and with eglantine.'

'Sweet are the uses of adversity.'

'Uneasy lies the head that wears a crown.'

'There is a tide in the affairs of men,
Which, taken at the flood, lead to fortune.
Omitted, all the voyage of their life
Is bound in shallows and in miseries.'

'How sharper than the serpent's tooth it is
To have a thankless child.'

'Methought I heard a voice cry "Sleep no more".'

'Put out the light, and then put out the light.'

'That England, that was wont to conquer others,
Hath made a shameful conquest of itself.'

'And every tale condemns me for a villain.'

'Good night, good night! Parting is such sweet sorrow
That I shall say good night till it be morrow.'

'The quality of mercy is not strained,
It droppeth as the gentle rain from heaven
Upon the place beneath.'

'O, what a world of vile ill-favoured faults
Looks handsome in three hundred pounds a year!'

'Who is Silvia? what is she,
That all our swains commend her?'

'If music be the food of love, play on;
Give me excess of it, that, surfeiting,
The appetite may sicken and so die.'

You'll find the answers in the pages that follow

ALL'S WELL THAT ENDS WELL

Written in 1602-03 and performed in the same years. The source is apparently a story of *'Decameron'* translated into English by William Painter.

Helena is the orphaned daughter of a famous physician, and is the ward of the Countess of Rousillon. Helena loves Bertram, the Countess's son. Bertram is summoned to the court of the sick King of France, and is accompanied by cowardly Parolles and loyal Lord Lafeu.

Helena follows Bertram and cures the king, and as a reward is allowed to choose one of the courtiers as a husband. Naturally she chooses Bertram, who objects to the marriage and escapes to the Tuscan Wars immediately after the marriage without having consummated it to Helena's satisfaction.

Helena returns to Rousillon, and then receives a letter from Bertram, promising to accept her if she can get a ring off his finger and give him a child. She disguises herself as a pilgrim and goes to Florence where her husband is courting Diana, a widow's daughter.

Helena persuades Diana to go to bed with Bertram, and to ask for the ring as a token. She takes Diana's place under cover of darkness, obtains the ring, and gives him one in exchange.

Bertram has been led to believe that Helena is dead so the loyal Lafeu arranges for Bertram to marry his daughter. However, the ring he gives his daughter is Helena's and the king recognises it. Bertram is arrested and so is Diana (she has arrived to accuse him of seduction) and it is not until Diana's mother turns up with a pregnant Helena wearing Bertram's ring that Bertram accepts his wife's persistence and the play ends satisfactorily.

Not a real favourite, for it implies a challenge to romanticism as the basis for marriage. The plot is thin and the verse uneven.

> 'Love all, trust a few,
> Do wrong to none; be able for thine enemy
> Rather in power than use, and keep thy friend
> Under thy own life's key; be check'd for silence,
> But never tax'd for speech.'
>
> The Countess of Rousillon

HE INSPIRED GREAT POETS

Giovanni Boccaccio (1315-1375), the Italian writer and humanist, was born near Florence. He was the son of a Florentine merchant. Most of his early years were spent in Naples, in literary study and writing. He moved in aristocratic circles and then returned to Florence in 1340. There he witnessed the ravages of The Black Death in 1348, which he described in the introduction to the first day of *'The Decameron'*. This was a collection of tales which he drew from many sources. They took him many years to write, and he assembled them finally between 1349 and 1351.

The tales are based upon the plague in 1348, when seven young ladies and three young men leave the city for neighbouring villas. Boccaccio describes the beauty of the villas and the young people amuse each other by telling tales in turn. They stay for 10 days, telling one tale each per day, so that the 100 tales are finally assembled.

'The Decameron' was translated by William Painter (c1525-95), and called *'Palace of Pleasure',* which gives some indication of the nature of the tales. *'Palace of Pleasure'*, is a collection of translations into English of *'Pleasant Histories and excellent Novells ... out of divers good and commendable Authors'*. It was published in 1566, 1567 and 1575, and it provided a great source of plots for Elizabethan writers. Shakespeare probably used one of the tales for *'All's Well That Ends Well'*, and for the *'Rape of Lucrece'*.

After 1350 Boccaccio was employed by the municipality of Florence on various diplomatic missions. He met and became friends with Petrarch (1304-1374) who was also a humanist. This gave a great impetus to Boccaccio's classical studies, and his house became an important centre of humanist activity. He wrote a *'Life of Dante'* (1265-1321), and delivered a course of lectures on the text of *'Divina Commedia'* (1373-74).

His chief works, apart from *'The Decameron',* were: *Filocolo*, a prose romance embodying the story of Floris and Blancheflour*; Filostrato*, a poem on the story of Troilus and Cressida; *Teseida*, a poem on the story of Theseus, Palamon and Arcite, which was translated by Chaucer in the *'Knight's Tale'; 'Ameto'*, a combination of allegory and pastoral romance; the *Amorosa Visione,* an uncompleted allegorical poem; *Fiammetta*, a psychological romance in prose, in which the woman herself recounts the various phases of her unhappy love; *'The Ninfale Fiesolano'*, an idyll translated into English by John Goubourne, an Elizabethan.

Boccaccio also wrote a number of encyclopaedic works in Latin which were widely read in England: *'The Genealogia Deorum';* the *'De Claris Mulieribus';* and *'De Casibus Girorum Illustrium',* this last being a source book for references to tragedy by Chaucer, by Lydgate in *'The Fall of Princes'* and for other stories.

In the history of literature, particularly of narrative fiction, Boccaccio is an important figure and among poets (other than Shakespeare) who found inspiration in his works were Chaucer (c1343-1400), Dryden (1631-1700), Keats (1795-1821), Longfellow (1807-82) and Tennyson (1809-92).

A MIDSUMMER NIGHT'S DREAM

Written in 1595 and performed 1595-96. Shakespeare probably drew from various sources, including Chaucer and Ovid.

Hermia is ordered by her father Egeus to marry Demetrius. But she loves Lysander, so refuses. In any case Demetrius loves Helena (Hermia's friend) and Helena returns the love.

Shakespeare has created an immediate problem. Theseus, The Duke, gives Hermia four days in which to obey her father. If she does not she dies or goes into a nunnery which, some might say, is a death of a different kind.

Hermia and Lysander leave Athens secretly, so that they can be married where Athenian law cannot trouble them. They are to meet in the woods a few miles from Athens.

Naturally Hermia tells Helena, who tells Demetrius, so they all end up in that part of the wood which is a favourite haunt of the fairies. There in the wood the King and Queen of the Fairies, Oberon and Titania, have quarrelled (unusual with fairies) because Titania refuses to give him a changeling as a page. (A changeling is a child secretly changed for another by elves, as the word implies).

Puck enters the scene. He's a mischievous little sprite and Oberon tells him to find a certain magic flower which, when the juice is squeezed onto Titania's eyes, will make her fall in love with whatever, whichever or whoever she sets her eyes upon when she wakens.

Result? Even more confusion! Now both Lysander and Demetrius are attracted to Helena, Hermia is cross, both ladies have a 'spirited' argument, and the men go off to fight for Helena. This is, of course, a Midsummer Night's Dream, and therefore not necessarily to be believed.

Oberon is still pursuing his objective, which is to get the love-invigorating juice onto Titania's eyelids. He succeeds. She wakes, and lo and behold she sees a weaver with an ass's head on him. She falls in love with him immediately (strange things are always so fascinating) and plays with his 'amiable cheeks' and 'fair large ears'. Some local tradespeople are rehearsing a play in the woods and Puck (it would be him) puts an ass's head on Bottom's head.

Mischievous sprite!

Titania's husband turns up. That's Oberon, the King. He's very cross. He reproaches Titania and demands the changeling boy once again. Titania gives him up to her husband in some confusion. Oberon then releases her from the love-charm. He is King, after all.

He also plays King once again. He instructs Puck to throw a thick fog around the woods, so that the humans, Lysander and Demetrius, Hermia and Helena, find themselves together (or rather lose themselves separately) and fall asleep close to each other without being aware of anyone else's presence.

The remedy to the love-potion is applied to their eyes, they awake, return to reason, and are reconciled with their loved ones with the aid of Puck, the original Marriage Guidance Counsellor. Hermia's father turns up, and so does Duke Theseus by some strange 'playwright's licence'. The fugitives are forgiven and are married to their chosen loved ones. The play ends with 'Pyramus and Thisbe' being acted by Bottom and his fellow tradesmen to the amusement of all.

How Shakespeare must have laughed to himself as he put that together in 1595 without the aid of gas, electricity or even a pencil torch!

> *'I know a bank whereon the wild thyme blows,*
> *Where oxlips and the nodding violet grows,*
> *Quite over-canopied with luscious woodbine,*
> *With sweet muskroses, and with eglantine.'*
>
> Oberon

ANTONY AND CLEOPATRA

Written and performed in 1607-08. The source of this tragedy is Sir Thomas North's translation of Plutarch, and much of the language is said to be extracted from it.

Antony is a Roman triumvir (a group of three leading men). Lepidus and Octavian are the other two. Whilst in Alexandria he becomes infatuated with Cleopatra and neglects his duties.

He hears of his wife's death (Fulvia) and a rebellion by Pompey, and despite Cleopatra's pleas he decides to return to Rome with his loyal general Enobarbus. The triumvirate is patched up and Antony agrees to marry Octavius's sister, Octavia. Pompey, too, accepts peace terms.

Cleopatra, when she hears of the news of Antony's marriage, furiously beats the messenger.

Antony is in Athens with Octavia when he hears that Octavius has sent an army against Pompey. Octavia returns to Rome to try to organise peace between her brother and her husband, and Antony returns to Egypt – and to Cleopatra. He is now fully committed to Egyptian opulence. His Roman discipline has deserted him.

Despite Enobarbus's advice Antony, now attacked by Octavius, joins with the Egyptian fleet to defend Egypt. At Actium, Cleopatra's ships flee and Antony follows her to Egypt.

Enobarbus deserts Antony, and Antony suffers a land defeat through the defection of the Egyptian Army.

Cleopatra, realising that she is now overtaken by Roman strength, hides in her monument. She sends a message to Antony to say that she is dead and Antony, defeated in battle and despairing because love has destroyed him, falls upon his sword.

He dies in Cleopatra's arms in her monument.

Cleopatra will inevitably be humiliated by Octavius. She therefore arranges for deadly asps to be smuggled into her monument, dresses in her finest robes and holds the asps to her body. Octavius has been outwitted and allows her body to be buried with that of Antony.

This is one of Shakespeare's great tragedies, for it combines beauty and desire and their conflict with politics and war.

As a great dramatist he would have been a fine director for the Antony and Cleopatra of Richard Burton and Elizabeth Taylor and would, no doubt, have welcomed it as a perpetuation of his stage production, first performed in 1607 when cameras, film and TV screens were probably not even imagined.

'The barge she sat in, like burnish'd throne,
Burn'd on the water. The poop was beaten gold;
Purple the sails, and so perfumed that
The winds were love-sick with them; the oars were silver,
Which to the tune of flutes kept stroke, and made
The water which they beat to follow faster,
As amorous of their strokes. For her own person,
It beggar'd all description.'

Enobarbus

THE QUEEN OF EGYPT

Cleopatra (69-30 BC) was the last and most famous of the Macedonian dynasty of the Ptolemies. She bore three children, and Antony admitted his paternity. Her ambition was probably to achieve the restoration of Ptolemaic power to the heights it had once reached under Ptolemy II Philadelphus.

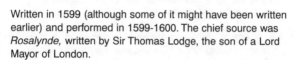

AS YOU LIKE IT

Written in 1599 (although some of it might have been written earlier) and performed in 1599-1600. The chief source was *Rosalynde,* written by Sir Thomas Lodge, the son of a Lord Mayor of London.

The plot is improved by entertainment and a number of songs. *'Under the Greenwood Tree'* is one. Thomas Hardy wrote a novel with that title. Another song is *'Blow, blow, thou winter wind'.*

Frederick has taken over the kingdom of his brother, who is a duke. The duke is surviving in the Forest of Arden with some faithful followers. Celia is Frederick's daughter, and both of them live at Frederick's court.

Rosalind falls in love with Orlando, the son of Rowland de Boys, when she sees him win a wrestling match. When Orlando's father died he had been left in the charge of his elder brother Oliver, and left home because of Oliver's cruelty towards him.

Orlando's father had been a friend of the duke whom Frederick had usurped, and therefore it was natural that Frederick, when he heard of Rosalind's love for Orlando, should expel Rosalind from his court.

As Celia and Rosalind were close friends it was also natural that Celia felt obliged to accompany her.

Rosalind now pretends to be Ganymede, a young countryman, and Celia pretends to be his sister Aliena. They meet Orlando again. He has joined Frederick's brother, the duke.

Rosalind entices Orlando (whilst still pretending to be Ganymede) to pay suit to her, and meanwhile Oliver, Orlando's cruel brother, comes to the forest to kill Orlando.

Fortunately Orlando saves him from a lioness and Oliver is therefore overcome with remorse.

He falls in love with Aliena and the wedding is arranged for the next day in the forest. Gretna Green was too far in those days.

Ganymede (Rosalind) being a clever young person assures Orlando that he (she) will produce his beloved Rosalind at the same time, so that Orlando can be married.

All are assembled with the banished duke to celebrate the double nuptials, and then Celia and Rosalind, having timed everything to perfection, put off their disguises and appear as they really are.

Marriages and celebrations follow and, to cap everything, news arrives that Frederick, who had set out with the intention of destroying the duke and his followers, has been converted by 'an old religious man'.

> *'Sweet are the uses of adversity:*
> *Which like a toad, ugly and venomous,*
> *Wears yet a precious jewel in his head:*
> *And this our life, exempt from public haunt,*
> *Finds tongues in trees, books in the running brooks,*
> *Sermons in stones, and good in everything.'*

Duke Senior

HE WAS WILD!

Sir Thomas Lodge (c1558-1625) was born in West Ham. He went to Merchant Taylors' School, then to Trinity College, Oxford, and in 1578 to Lincoln's Inn.

In 1588 he took part in a buccaneering expedition to the Canaries.

Among his writings was *'Rosalynde'* (1590) which supplied Shakespeare with many of the major incidents in *'As You Like It'*.

CORIOLANUS

Written and performed in 1607-08. Shakespeare's main source for this tragedy was a translation of Plutarch's '*Lives*' by Sir Thomas North.

This is one of the plays Shakespeare wrote based upon Rome and Roman life. He had already written '*Julius Caesar*' and '*Antony and Cleopatra*'. In '*Coriolanus*', Shakespeare draws attention to the domestic demands of the people on those who rule them.

The plebeians were the common people of Rome and the patricians the ancient Roman nobles. When the play opens the plebeians are about to rebel against their patrician rulers. Menenius Agrippa persuades the plebeians to work for the common good, but Caius Martius angers them with his arrogance.

Fortunately, an immediate crisis is averted by the appointment of Five Tribunes of The People, and by a Volscian uprising to which Caius Martius is sent in order to suppress it.

Caius Martius captures Corioli, a Volscian city, and returns to Rome to a great welcome. He is named Coriolanus and promptly elected to the Senate. However, this necessitates an acceptance of the traditional rites of public humility. It is too much for the proud Coriolanus and he is not supported by the Tribunes.

Coriolanus has a sworn enemy in the Volscian leader Tullus Aufidius, and the latter plans another attack on Rome. Coriolanus's mother, Volumnia, persuades him to ask the plebeians for their support but he is too proud.

The Tribunes eventually demand banishment, so Coriolanus offers his services to his enemy, Tullus Aufidius, as an ally or a sacrifice. He becomes the leader of the Volscian army against Rome and although the Senators plead with him he is only persuaded to spare Rome when his mother confronts him.

Aufidius feels betrayed and Coriolanus is killed by the Volscians as the enemy he proved to be.

The play is political and tragic, and expresses conflict between rule and ruled.

> '*If you have writ your annals true, 'tis there*
> *That, like an eagle in a dove-cote, I*
> *Flutter'd your Volscians in Corioli,*
> *Alone I did it.*'
>
> Coriolanus

PLUTARCH, THE GREEK

Ploutarchos Plutarch (c46-c120) was an historian, biographer and philosopher. His education began in Athens, and he visited Rome often, once as Chargé d'Affaires of his native town.

In Rome he gave public lectures in philosophy.

He was born in Chaeronia, in Boeotia, and there he spent all his mature life.

He is best known for his *'Parallel Lives'*. Other works are historical, and many are grouped under the general head of *'Opera Moralia'*.

'Parallel Lives' contains a selection of 46 of the great characters preceding his own age. Each was published in successive books, each pair forming one book, a Greek and a Roman, with some resemblance between their respective careers. Some of the sequels, giving detailed comparisons of each warrior, statesman, legislator or hero, are regarded as spurious by critics.

But history can never be entirely accurate.

In his *'Heros and Hero-Worship'*, Thomas Carlyle (1795-1881) wrote: 'History is a distillation of rumour'. Plutarch's *'Biographies'* are monuments of great literary value, containing precious material based upon lost records.

He always maintained his professed purpose – portraiture of character. He omits or briefly touches upon the most famous actions or events which distinguish the career of each of his subjects.

Plutarch believed that a man's virtues or failings are best shown through some trifling incident, word or jest.

'The Morals' are a collection of short treatises. There were 60 of them, and they dealt with Ethics, Politics, History, Health, Facetiae, Love-stories, Philosophy and 'Isis and Osiris'. There is a Christian spirit in some of them, although the author probably knew nothing of Christianity.

His *'Symposiaca'* (Table-talk) shows him as an amiable and genial companion and in his dialogue *'Gryllus'* he reveals a remarkable sense of humour. Plutarch was a man of rare gifts, even though he may not have been a profound thinker.

Biographers write about the lives of others, and presumably do not have to be profound themselves. Was Boswell an example? Plutarch occupies a rare place in literature as a chronicler, an encyclopaedist of antiquity.

Sir Thomas North (c1535-c1601) was the son of Sir Edward North, the 1st Baron. In 1579 he translated Plutarch, and it is from his translations that Shakespeare drew his knowledge of ancient history. The translations were, in fact, the major source for Shakespeare's Roman plays.

For many young students of Shakespeare it is difficult to understand how Shakespeare could have known so much. He was writing plays for the London stage, and was brilliant enough to dramatise in remarkable histrionic language the plays that are now accepted as the greatest presentations of human life on the stage ever conceived and written. Shakespeare was, of course, an actor, a playwright and a dramatist. He was able to combine those three talents on an English stage on a 'sceptred isle'.

How Plutarch must have excited him!

CYMBELINE

Written and performed 1609-10. The sources for the plot are Holinshed's, *'A Mirror for Magistrates'* and possibly Boccaccio's *'Decameron'*.

The play was criticised by Dr. Samuel Johnson for its illogicality, but Tennyson died with a copy of it on his bed and therefore must have been interested in the content. And Shaw wrote an amended version of the Fifth Act which he called *'Cymbeline Refinished'*.

Cymbeline is the King of Britain. He has a daughter, Imogen, who has secretly married Leonatus Posthumus 'a poor but worthy gentleman'. The Queen of England is Imogen's stepmother. She has a clownish son, Colten, and is determined that he shall marry Imogen.

Whilst in Rome, Posthumus boasts of Imogen's virtue to a certain Iachimo and wagers that if Iachimo can seduce Imogen he will give him a diamond ring, a gift from Imogen.

However, Iachimo is repulsed by Imogen. He hides in her bedroom and is able to pass to Posthumus details of her room and body which made Posthumus believe that Imogen is unfaithful. Posthumus gives Iachimo the ring he promised him.

Posthumus decides to kill Imogen and writes to his servant Pisanio with instructions to do the dirty deed. But instead Pisanio sends a bloody cloth to Posthumus to make him think the deed is done and provides Imogen with a male disguise.

Imogen assumes the name Fidele and becomes a page to Bellarius and Cymbeline's two lost sons – Guiderius and Arviragus. They are living in a cave in Wales. Fidele (Imogen) becomes ill and the brothers find her and believe she is dead.

When they leave her as dead she recovers to find, at her side, the headless corpse of Cloten. Because he is wearing Posthumus' borrowed clothing she believes it is her husband. Naturally, with a head missing it is difficult to recognise him.

A Roman army invades Britain and Imogen becomes the page of Lucius, a Roman general. The Britons defeat the Romans through valour shown by Bellarius, aided by the disguised Posthumus, but Posthumus is taken prisoner (he is disguised as a Roman) and has a vision whilst in gaol.

Lucius, the Roman general, pleads with Cymbeline for the life of Fedele (Imogen) and Cymbeline, who is moved by something familiar about her (she is his daughter, of course), spares her life and grants her a special favour.

The favour she requests is that Iachimo should tell how he came by the ring he is wearing. Posthumus hears of the confession by Iachimo, and because he now knows she is faithful and yet is dead he is in despair.

Then Imogen reveals herself. The king is overjoyed at recovering his daughter. He is further overjoyed (if that's possible) by the return of his two sons, and everything ends in great reconciliation all round.

Tennyson described Posthumus' words to Imogen when he became reconciled to her as 'the tenderest lines in Shakespeare'.

And the lines?

> *'Hang there like fruit, my soul,*
> *Till the tree die'*

Is it any wonder that although originally regarded as a tragedy in the First Folio, it is now regarded as one of Shakespeare's romances?

> *'Hark, hark! the lark at heaven's gate sings,*
> *And Phoebus 'gins arise'*
> *His steeds to water at those springs*
> *In chalic'd flow'rs that lies:*
> *And winking Mary-buds begin*
> *To ope their golden eyes.*
> *With everything that pretty is,*
> *My lady sweet, arise:*
> *Arise, arise!'*
>
> A song from Cymbeline

HAMLET

Written and performed 1600-01.

The Prince of Denmark, a tragedy, was probably unfamiliar to Elizabethan audiences when Shakespeare wrote his play.

Hamlet is regarded as Shakespeare's finest dramatic play. He had written great comedies and historical plays, and this preceded his production of the great tragedies –'Othello', 'King Lear', and 'Macbeth'.

King Hamlet has died, and his brother Claudius is now the King of Denmark. Furthermore, Claudius has married King Hamlet's widow, Gertrude. Prince Hamlet, somewhat deranged by his father's death and his mother's quick remarriage, believes his friend, Horatio, when he is told that his father's ghost is haunting the battlements.

Hamlet decides to watch with Horatio. The ghost appears and tells Hamlet that Claudius poisoned him. Is it genuine? Hamlet is uncertain. Besides, he needs to confirm his own mother's innocence if the ghost is telling the truth.

A company of actors arriving at the Danish court provide the setting for this dénouement. Hamlet is able to persuade the actors to present a play which is parallel to the present situation – Claudius's possible poisoning of his father and his mother's complicity in the act.

Polonius, the court chamberlain, is now convinced that Prince Hamlet is mad, because of his strange behaviour towards Ophelia, the daughter of Polonius.

When the play is performed Claudius gives himself away, and orders Hamlet to England where he plans to have him killed.

Hamlet escapes, confronts his mother in her chamber, and believing Claudius is eaves-dropping behind the arras he stabs him to death. it is Polonius!

Laertes, Polonius' son, is determined to avenge his father's death and returns to Denmark. There he finds his sister, Ophelia, mad. Claudius hears that Hamlet is back in Denmark. He plots a duel where Laertes will be equipped with a poison-tipped sword, and the fact that Ophelia has died by drowning strengthens Laertes' resolve to kill Hamlet.

The duel finally takes place, and Gertrude dies, Laertes dies, Claudius dies – and eventually Hamlet dies in that final dramatic death scene. The play ends with Fortinbras, the King of Norway, being proclaimed King of Denmark, and ordering a military funeral for Prince Hamlet.

Great actors have played Hamlet and will again. They will be forgotten, Shakespeare's tragedy and his dramatic poetry will not.

> *'O, that this too too solid flesh would melt,*
> *Thaw and resolve itself into dew!*
> *Or that the Everlasting had not fix'd*
> *His canon against self-slaughter! O God! God!*
> *How weary, stale, flat, and unprofitable,*
> *Seem to me all the uses of this world!'*

Hamlet

Tom Stoppard and Hamlet

Not Hamlet himself! It was Tom Stoppard's *'Rosencrantz and Guildenstern Are Dead'* that dovetailed neatly with Shakespeare's play.

It was first performed at the Edinburgh Festival in 1966, and then in revised form at the National Theatre in London in 1967. The eponymous heroes puzzle over their own identities, and their own relationship to the events at Elsinore. Witty, artistic and philosophic.

Just another tribute to Shakespeare.

HENRY IV PART I

Written in 1596 and performed 1597-98.

The chief sources are the '*Chronicles*' of Hall and Holinshed. In 1640 Leonard Digges recorded the popularity of the play, 24 years after Shakespeare's death. All Shakespeare's historical plays have been popular since, although reading them is, of course, the most popular pursuit of all.

The subject of Henry IV, Part I, is the rebellion of the Percys, together with Owen Glendower and Mortimer, and assisted by Douglas. The King and Prince Hal (The Prince of Wales) overcome the rebellion at Shrewsbury in 1403.

The Prince of Wales leads a riotous life with Falstaff and his companions – Poins, Bardoph and Peto. The Prince and Poins organise a plan for the others to rob travellers at Gadshill, and then for the robbers to be robbed themselves! Strange goings on which lead to Falstaff's own version of his implication in the affair.

At the Battle of Shrewsbury the Prince of Wales (Hal) kills Hotspur in single combat, finds Falstaff pretending to be dead, and mourns him with the words 'I could be better spar'd a better man'.

Falstaff claims credit for killing Hotspur, and Shakespeare proves himself a great comedy playwright in his creation of Falstaff and his use of dramatic irony.

Falstaff:

> And is not my hostess of the tavern a most sweet wench?

Prince:

> As the honey of Hybla, my old lad of the castle.

Falstaff and Prince Hal

Nevillle Chamberllain quoted from this play on his return from Munich in 1938:
'Out of this nettle, danger, we pluck this flower, safety.'
The following year there was war with the danger – Germany!

HENRY IV PART II

Written in 1597 and performed 1597-98.

A continuation of the Falstaff theme and now introducing the Prince of Wales as king upon his father's death.

In this play it is Archbishop Scroop, Mowbray and Hastings who rebel. Falstaff's comical activities are continued with the support of Pistol, Poins, Mistress Quickly, and Doll Tearsheet.

Falstaff falls in with Justices Shallow and Silence whilst recruiting for his beloved Hal, and even manages to extract £1,000 from the former Justice.

Henry IV dies, having been reconciled with his somewhat dissolute son.

Falstaff hurries from Gloucestershire to greet Hal, now King Henry V of England, only to be rejected with the speech beginning, 'I know thee not, old man. Fall to thy prayers'.

Falstaff is banished from the king's presence. Prince Hal is now king.

> *'Canst thou, O partial sleep, give thy repose*
> *To the wet sea-boy in an hour so rude;*
> *And in the calmest and most stillest night,*
> *With all appliances and means to boot,*
> *Deny it to a king! Then, happy low, lie down!*
> *Uneasy lies the head that wears a crown.'*

Henry IV

WAS FALSTAFF REAL?

Yes, he was probably based upon Sir John Oldcastle (c1378-1417) who commanded an English army in France, and forced the Duc D'Orleans to lift the seige of Paris. There was a popular tradition of dislike for Sir John, and he was finally hanged for holding heretical views. He paid preachers to promote his views, after having Wycliffe's works transcribed and distributed.

HENRY V

Written in 1599 and performed the same year.

Shakespeare's main source was Holinshed's '*Chronicles*'. He may also have consulted Edward Hall's '*The Union of the Two Noble and Illustre Families of Lancastre and York*'.

Without Falstaff there is a lack of comedy, but as this is a patriotic play Shakespeare knew his audience well. In any event, Shakespeare had already written '*The Merry Wives of Windsor*' to satisfy the great public demand for Falstaff.

Henry V was Falstaff's 'Hal' and therefore was mocked by the French who knew his exploits as a young prince. But he first quells a rebellion at home before proving his military prowess in France, especially at Agincourt. King Henry V is even romantic enough to woo Katherine, the French princess, and seal their marriage vows with a kiss. How the audience must have loved it.

Hal's old pals (Pistol, Bardolph and Nym) appear in a subplot, and Henry's kingdom now includes four commanders to be by his side. They are Gower for England, Fluellen for Wales, Macmorris for Ireland, and Jamie for Scotland.

Laurence (Lord) Olivier made *Henry V* known to most people through his great film. Shakespeare made it known by that great speech:

> '*Once more unto the breach, dear friends, once more;*
> *Or close the wall up with our English dead!*
> *In peace there's nothing so becomes a man*
> *As modest stillness and humility:*
> *But when the blast of war blows in our ears,*
> *Then imitate the action of the tiger.*'
> *Stiffen the sinews, summon up the blood,*
> *Disguise fair nature with hard-favour'd range;*
> *Then lend the eye a terrible aspect*'.

Henry V

HENRY VI PART 1

May date from as early as 1590 and from the same source as *Henry V*. Although Shakespeare was the main author it is considered that he was not the sole one.

The play opens with the funeral of Henry V, and introduces the subsequent wars with France and Joan of Arc, and the establishment of the Wars of the Roses.

The conflict between Plantagenet and York is brought into the open by the plucking of the red and the white rose in the Temple garden.

Nowadays the Wars of the Roses are repeated peaceably between Lancashire and Yorkshire Cricket Elevens (those are in alphabetical order, not necessarily in order of superiority) on fields where great cricketers have since battled with bat and ball.

Plantagenet:

> *Let him that is a true-born gentleman,*
> *And stands upon the honour of his birth,*
> *If he suppose that I have pleaded truth,*
> *From off this brier pluck a white rose with me.*

Somerset:

> *Let him that is no coward nor no flatterer;*
> *But dare maintain the party of the truth,*
> *Pluck a red rose from off the thorn with me.*

Plantagenet and Somerset

Those 'Rose Wars' Lasted 30 Years

The first of the many battles between the Houses of York and Lancaster took place at St. Albans in 1455. The Yorkists were victors.

The last was in 1485 on Bosworth Field where Richard III was killed. Henry VII, the victor, became the first Tudor king of England.

HENRY VI PART II

Published anonymously in 1594 under the title '*The First Part of the Contention betwixt the two famous Houses of Yorke and Lancaster*'. The Fifth Act of Henry VI, Part I, was concerned with the arrangement by the Earl of Suffolk of a marriage between young Henry VI with Margaret of Anjou, daughter of the King of Naples. Part II opens with that marriage.

Humphrey, the Duke of Gloucester, was appointed by Lord Protector of young Henry VI upon Henry V's death. He was the youngest son of Henry IV, and acted as Regent until 1431 in place of his brother, the Duke of Bedford, whilst Bedford was in France making war most of the time.

In this play Humphrey is angered by the marriage arranged between his 'ward' and Margaret of Anjou. Unfortunately his wife Eleanor apparently practised witchcraft, and she was imprisoned in the Isle of Man in 1446.

Humphrey is arrested on a charge of high treason, against the king's better judgement, and murdered. Suffolk is banished, and after saying farewell to Queen Margaret he is murdered by pirates on the Kent coast.

The play is concerned with the dynastic struggle between the two roses, so the complex plots and counterplots (John le Carré could not have done better) make the play confused. Episodes and characters make the play memorable.

Richard, Duke of York, is a pretender to the throne and stirs up Jack Cade to rebellion in Act IV. Cade is killed by Alexander Iden, a Kentish gentleman, and the final Act is concerned with the Battle of St. Albans. Somerset is killed, a victory for the Yorkists but not, it must be noted, on the playing fields of Old Trafford or Headingley.

Cade:
There shall be in England seven halfpenny loaves sold for a penny;
the three-hooped pot shall have ten hoops;
and I shall make it felony to drink small beer.
All the realm shall be in common, and in Cheapside shall my palfrey go to grass. And when I am king, – as king I will be, –
... there shall be no money; all shall eat and drink on my score; and I will apparel them all in one livery, that they may agree like brothers, and worship me their lord.
Dick:
The first thing we do, let's kill all the lawyers.

Cade and Dick

HENRY VI PART III

Full of sound and fury, signifying everything, to misquote one of Shakespeare's famous lines in Macbeth!

The play opens with Henry VI attempting to make peace (between those roses) by making the Duke of York his heir. It means that he will disinherit his son by Margaret.

So Margaret investigates the murder of the boy Rutland, the Duke of York's youngest son, by Clifford, and York himself is murdered. At the battle of Towton, Clifford is killed.

There is a scene where a son who has killed his father encounters a father who has killed his son!

Henry VI is captured in this play and Edward IV is proclaimed king. He marries the widow, Elizabeth Gray, although having been promised to Bonner, the French king's sister. The mayhem progresses when Richard, Duke of Gloucester (later to become Richard III) begins to indicate his ambitions.

The Earl of Warwick, a Lancastrian kingmaker, is killed at Barnet by King Edward. At the Battle of Tewkesbury, King Edward has a decisive victory. Margaret's young son, also an Edward, is killed in cold blood, and finally King Henry, who is imprisoned in the Tower of London, is murdered by Richard.

Shakespeare's *Richard III* (remember Olivier?) was a play where the dramatist 'wrapped up' this historical tetralogy which, although not often performed on the stage, are fascinating plays to read.

> '*O, God! me thinks it were a happy life*
> *To be no better than a homely swain;*
> *To sit upon a hill, as I do now,*
> *To carve out dials, quaintly, point by point,*
> *Thereby to see the minutes how they run.*
> *How many make the hour full complete,*
> *How many hours bring about the day;*
> *How many days will finish up the year;*
> *How many years a mortal man may live.*'

Henry VI

HENRY VIII

Written in 1613 and performed in the same year.

Tennyson attributed much of this play to J. Fletcher and as Shakespeare was now 49 years of age, and within three years of his death, it is likely that he was collaborating with other authors in his declining years.

The play deals with the fall and execution of the Duke of Buckingham, the royal divorce, Cardinal Wolsey and his death, the coronation of Anne Boleyn, Cranmer's triumph over his enemies, and the christening of the Princess Elizabeth – later to become Queen Elizabeth I.

At the time of the production of this play, Queen Elizabeth had been dead for ten years.

> 'Farewell! a long farewell, to all my greatness!
> This is the state of man: today he puts forth
> The tender leaves of hope; tomorrow blossoms,
> And bears his blushing honours thick upon him;
> The third day comes a frost, a killing frost;
> And, when he thinks, good easy man, full surely
> His greatness is a-ripening, nips his root,
> And then he falls, as I do.'
>
> Cardinal Wolsey

THE KING EXECUTIONER

He could have been a Hollywood film star! He had six wives, two of whom he executed, two of whom he divorced and the other two finished up in limbo.

He broke with the Roman Church, and destroyed most of the remaining vestiges of the old religious establishment. The popularity of the play depended more upon the pictorial stage splendour and purple rhetoric than as a meritorious play. Henry VIII has been filmed a number of times because of that splendour.

JULIUS CAESAR

Written and performed in 1599. The major source for Shakespeare was North's translation of Plutarch's *'Lives'*.

A very popular play which opens in 44BC with the return to Rome of Julius Caesar.

He had completed a successful campaign in Spain and as he was already accepted as Dictator it is feared he might wish to be crowned king.

There is a conspiracy against him with Cassius and Caspar as the prime instigators.

They are lovers of freedom and gain the reluctant support of Brutus because of his sense of duty to the Republic.

The conspirators kill Caesar in the Senate House and Brutus, Caesar's friend, makes that great speech:

'Friends, Romans, and Countrymen, lend me your ears'

This stirs the people against the conspirators, and Octavius (Caesar's nephew), Antony and Lepidus, who are united as triumvirs, oppose Brutus and Cassius.

When they hear the news of Portia's death (she is Brutus' wife) there is a reconciliation between Brutus and Cassius, but they meet finally at the Battle of Philippi (42BC) and kill themselves.

> *'There is a tide in the affairs of men,*
> *Which, taken at the flood, lead to fortune;*
> *Omitted, all the voyage of their life*
> *Is bound in shallows and in miseries.*
> *On such a full sea are we now afloat,*
> *And we must take the current when it serves,*
> *Or lose our ventures.'*

Brutus

KING JOHN

Written in 1590-91 and performed 1596-97.

Supposed to be a piece of theatrical cobbling, as it does not mention the signing of the Magna Carta!

Shakespeare was only 27 when this was cobbled and therefore it was one of his early plays.

King John is determined to keep his throne, although his young nephew, Arthur, has stronger claims. Arthur has the support of the King of France apart from a more legitimate succession from John's older brother, Geoffrey.

John bribes Hubert de Burgh to blind Arthur. He is beset by the French, Arthur's mother Constance, and by Cardinal Pandulph, the papal legate.

In a memorable scene, Arthur's pleas affect Hubert so deeply that he spares him, but later in the play Arthur, trying to escape, jumps to his death.

The French invade and John is defeated, taking refuge in Swinstead Abbey. He dies there, poisoned (it is presumed) by a monk.

The French troops return to their native land, leaving Cardinal Pandulph to arrange an honourable peace.

Henry III is the new king, and his responsibility is to restore England's equilibrium after the ravages of John's reign.

> *'To gild refined gold, to paint the lily,*
> *To throw a perfume on the violet,*
> *To smooth the ice, or add another hue*
> *Unto the rainbow, or with taper-light*
> *To seek the beauteous eye of heaven to garnish,*
> *Is wasteful and ridiculous excess.'*

Salisbury

John was so despised that the English barons forced him to sign the Magna Carta in 1215 at Runnemede in Berkshire. Later he ignored its provisions and died while on campaign.

AN OPEN LETTER TO WILLIAM SHAKESPEARE

Dear Mr. Shakespeare,

I write humbly, because while you sit amongst the immortals, flicking through the myriad pages of rapturous puff, universal hosannas and, occasionally, a hint of criticism, you may be planning a comeback!

Hint of criticism?

'With the single exception of Homer, there is no eminent writer, not even Sir Walter Scott, whom I can despise so entirely as I despise Shakespeare when I measure my mind against his.... It would positively be a relief to me to dig him up and throw stones at him.'

(George Bernard Shaw (1856-1950) in his 'Dramatic Opinions and Essays').

O, dear! And what about:

'Shakespeare never had six lines together without a fault. Perhaps you may find seven.'

(Dr. Samuel Johnson (1709-1784))

O, dear again!

But Dr. Johnson did praise you occasionally, and would not have thrown stones.

And what about all those who prefer Francis Bacon, Baron Verulam of Verulam, Viscount St. Albans (1561-1626), the English philosopher and statesman, born in London, who was the younger son of Sir Nicholas Bacon?

He entered Trinity College, Cambridge, was called to the bar in 1582, and was an MP in 1584. You were 20 at the time and decided to try your luck on the London stage. You already had three children by Anne Hathaway, and you were dependent upon your father.

There are some who say Bacon wrote your plays The comparison is odious.

You were 'an upstart crow', according to Robert Greene in 1595, while Bacon attached himself to the Earl of Essex, from whom he accepted a gift of land at Twickenham.

Perched on your lofty pinnacle in the 'Immortals' Pavilion', in the company of Mozart and Beethoven, perhaps? Cezanne? Michaelangelo? Leonardo da Vinci? W.G.Grace? (I'm not sure that you mention cricket), do you smile benignly at the hundreds of millions who throng the theatres throughout the world, enraptured by modern interpretations of *Hamlet, Macbeth, King Lear* – and even *Bottom*?

Do you recall that by 1592 (you were then 28) you had written *Henry VI* in three parts, *King John and Richard III, The Comedy of Errors, The Taming of the Shrew, The Two Gentlemen of Verona,* and *Titus Andronicus?*

You were a new star on stage, in theatrical management, in stage direction and in composing (in your spare time) plays which still attract large audiences. By 1598 you had written most of your sonnets, many of them now ranked amongst the world's finest poems.

After the plague in London, when the theatres reopened, you were in your element.

You had been a 'hired man'. now you were given shares in The Chamberlain's Men, and were able to receive the Queen's payment for the company's performances at court during the Christmas festivities of 1594-95.

What a remarkable career you had after that triumph.

Mr. Shakespeare, if (and when) you are reincarnated will you go straight to Hollywood on contract? Or will you go back to New Place (now Old Place and open to the public, of course). Or will you go back to Anne Hathaway's cottage (also open to the public).

Or will you, as a typical gesture, go back to London, to the Globe, where you can act again, write again, direct again, and perhaps meet your old pal, Richard Burbage?

THE EDITOR

KING LEAR

Written and performed 1605-6. Shakespeare used various sources, including Holinshed's 'Chronicles' and Sir Philip Sidney's *'Arcadia'*.

Shakespeare was 41 when he wrote this remarkable play. it may well be regarded as his greatest tragedy, depicting the rejection of parent by grown-up child.

King Lear plans to share his kingdom between his three daughters. He prefers to stay with them as a regular and honoured guest. His youngest daughter, Cordelia, does not join in the public declarations of love made by her two sisters and Lear angrily divides his kingdom between Goneril and Regan, his elder daughters.

Cordelia is given no dowry when she marries the King of France and leaves the country.

The king finds the daughters to whom he has given his kingdom accept him as a guest grudgingly, and in despair he wanders into heathland, accompanied by his Fool, and guided by the Duke of Kent, who is loyal to him. At the end of his tether he goes mad and realises how vulnerable he is without the power that was once his.

A French army lands and Lear is assisted by the Duke of Gloucester to Dover, where the king hopes to be reunited with Cordelia. Goneril, Regan and the Duke of Cornwall, (Regan's husband) torture and blind the Duke of Gloucester and the French army lose the battle.

Cordelia and Lear are captured, and the powerful Edmund (the Duke of Gloucester's bastard son, and lover of Goneril and Regan) orders that they be put to death.

Then Edmund is defeated in single combat by his legitimate brother, Edgar, and confesses to the act as he lies dying. His confession is too late to save Cordelia, and Lear comes on-stage carrying the corpse of his hanged daughter, asserting that she is still alive. He dies, mad once again.

The play carries a double plot of rejection and tragedy. Lear is rejected by his daughters, although Cordelia loves him, and the Duke of Gloucester rejects his legitimate son, Edgar, and wrongly trusts his illegitimate son, Edmund. It is Edgar who revenges his father by killing Edmund.

There is superb poetry in the play and the philosophical intuition of Shakespeare is constantly present, even in the melodramatic tragedy.

> *'How sharper than the serpent's tooth it is
> To have a thankless child.'*
>
> King Lear

Dramatis Personae

Lear – *King of Britain*
King of France
Duke of Burgundy
Duke of Cornwall
Duke of Albany
Earl of Kent
Earl of Gloster
Edgar – *Son of Gloster*
Edmund – *Bastard Son to Gloster*
Curan – *a Courtier*
Oswald – *Steward to Goneril*
Old Man – *Tenant to Gloster*
Physician
Fol
An Officer – *employed by Edmund*
Gentleman – *Attendant on Cordelia*
A Herald
Servants to Cornwall
Goneril, Regan, Cordelia – *Daughters to Lear*
Knights of Lear's Train, Officers, Messengers, Soldiers and Attendants

The play is set in Britain

LOVE'S LABOUR'S LOST

Written in 1588 and performed in 1595. The sources of this play have not been identified, and the play has been said to attack a coterie of free-thinkers dabbling in the occult and alchemy.

They include Raleigh and Marlowe, but the existence of such a circle is disputed.

The King of Navarre and a group of lords have vowed to keep from the sight of women and to live studying and fasting for three years. Try it yourself!

The Princess of France arrives on a mission, with her attendant ladies, and the king is soon in love with the Princess. At the same time his lords are soon in love with the ladies, and there follows much merriment whilst the courting proceeds, with disguises hiding real identities.

The proceedings are helped along with the assistance of Don Adriano de Armado, the Spaniard, who is a master of extravagant language, Holofernes the schoolmaster, Dull the constable, Sir Nathaniel the curate, and Costard the clown.

News arrives of the death of the Princess's father and this causes the ladies to impose a year's ordeal on their lovers. The play ends with the song:

> 'When icicles hang by the wall,
> And Dick, the shepherd, blows his nail,
> And Tom bears logs into the hall,
> And milk comes frozen home in pail,
> When blood is nipp'd and ways be foul,
> Then nightly sings the staring owl,
> To-who;
> Tu-whit, tu-who – a merry note,
> While greasy Joan doth keel the pot!'
>
> A song

THE ELIXIR OF LIFE

'Will was in his mid-twenties when he wrote Love's Labour's Lost. He had a wife and three small children in Stratford, and his father was in financial difficulties. He was developing a remarkable career for himself on stage (but not yet on screen!) writing plays and acting in some of them himself.

He was reading avidly and perhaps, while relaxing over an ale in a London tavern, he heard of Roger Bacon and Albertus Magnus. Perhaps he met someone who had read the writings of Paracelsus (16th century), the Swiss writer who was deeply interested in alchemy as a medical application for a chemical therapy to cure diseases.

Paracelsus and his followers were looking for the elixir of life, eternal youth! It was a dream world, far wider than the idea of converting base metals into gold, and the emergence of science gradually undermined alchemy and other forms of the occult.

In 1588 Shakespeare, who was a realist, probably recognised the fundamental error in the reasoning of the alchemists. Yet he was able to write in 1600 in 'Hamlet' the lines:

'There are more things in heaven and earth, Horatio,
Than are dream of in your philosophy'.

Loves' Labour's Lost appears to be one of the few plays Shakespeare created himself. That does not reduce the value of his other plays. 37 successful plays in 25 years, all packed with dramatic poetry quoted all over the world time and time again, is some going!

To compare anyone else to him is worse than odious!

Shakespeare was a realist and a genius. He was able to think about the ideas of other people, wrap them imaginatively into dramatic form, and help his colleagues to stage them successfully.

How remarkable it would have been if he had himself discovered the elixir of life, so that today, sitting quietly by his vast swimming pool, surrounded by a high wire fence and an army of security guards keeping the paparazzi away, he could dream up other great plays, and enjoy the interest on billions of pounds and dollars (and yen) that others now enjoy through his works.

What an impossible dream.

Perhaps in Love's Labour's Lost he knew it had to end. He retired at 48 and died at 52, never having discovered the elixir of life, except through his works.

MACBETH

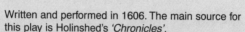

Written and performed in 1606. The main source for this play is Holinshed's *'Chronicles'*.

It is considered that Banquo is the legendary ancestor of James I and the Stuarts. Shakespeare intended this play to flatter James I, who was known to have an interest in witchcraft.

King Duncan of Scotland's army is rescued by the gallantry of his two generals – Macbeth and Banquo. As they are returning to the king they meet three witches, who prophecy that Macbeth will become Thane of Cawdor and King of Scotland, and that Banquo's sons will be kings.

Macbeth is indeed appointed Thane of Cawdor and he writes to his wife, informing her of Duncan's intention to visit them in their castle at Inverness. Lady Macbeth decides to have the king killed, and overrides Macbeth's reluctance.

She prepares an alibi for Macbeth so that the suspicion falls on Duncan's sons, Malcolm and Donalbain. Suspicion grows when they flee from Scotland.

Macbeth is now king but feels unsafe.

As the witches had prophesied that Banquo's sons would be kings, Macbeth resolves to have Banquo and his son killed, but the murderers bungle the task and Banquo's son escapes.

Unable to sleep, Macbeth consults the witches, and is assured that he will not be defeated until Birnam Wood comes to Dunsinane Castle, and that no man born of woman can harm him.

However, Macduff, the powerful Thane of Fife, seeks out Malcolm in England and Macbeth angrily orders the slaughter of Macduff's family.

Malcolm's army advances on Macbeth's castle. Lady Macbeth walks in her sleep, distracted by grief. She talks in her sleep, and betrays the secret of Duncan's murder.

Even Macbeth becomes isolated from her, and only the witches' assurance gives him courage.

Malcolm instructs his army to cut branches from Birnam Wood to use as camouflage, and Macbeth then realises that Birnam Wood is, indeed, coming to his castle.

He is killed by Macduff, having been told that Macduff was not born but was 'untimely ripped' from his mother's womb.

Malcolm is then placed on the Scottish throne by Macduff.

'Methought I heard a voice cry 'Sleep no more;
Macbeth does murder sleep' – the innocent sleep,
Sleep that knits up the ravell'd sleave of care,
The death of each day's life, sore labour's bath,
Balm of hurt minds, great nature's second course,
Chief nourisher in life's feast.'

Macbeth

O, THOSE THREE WITCHES

Scene 1 – An open place, with thunder and lightning

Witch 1	When shall we three meet again, In thunder, lightning or in rain?
Witch 2	When the hurlyburly's done, When the battle's lost and won.
Witch 3	That will be ere the set of sun.

A spectacular opening for a thriller!

MEASURE FOR MEASURE

This was formerly a comedy, but it is now classed among the 'problem plays'.

First performed c1604 and published in the First Folio of 1623.

Shakespeare's main source is George Whetstone's '*Promos and Cassandra*', a translation of a play by Cinthio.

Duke Vincentio is disturbed by the unruliness of Vienna, and resolves to absent himself from rule and leave law enforcement to Angelo, his puritanical deputy.

The Duke remains in Vienna disguised as a friar, in order to observe the consequences of his decision. Angelo orders the destruction of the brothels and, invoking a law against lechery, imprisons Claudio for making the woman to whom he is betrothed, pregnant. The penalty is death, so Claudio asks his sister, Isabella, who is a novice in a nunnery, to intercede.

Angelo is overcome by lust when he is confronted by Isabella, and offers Claudio's life in exchange for her body. Claudio begs her to accept the offer, but Isabella is outraged. However, she is persuaded by Vincentio (disguised, remember!) to play a trick on Angelo.

He tells her that Angelo had broken a marriage contract with a certain Mariana because Mariana had lost her dowry. Mariana was mourning her lost love, and would willingly take Isabella's place in Angelo's bed.

It is all arranged, but Angelo decides to have Claudio killed despite his promise to Isabella.

Fortunately, a pirate with a physical resemblance to Claudio gives Duke Vincentio another opportunity to thwart Angelo, and the latter's villainy is unmasked when the duke makes an 'unexpected return' to Vienna.

Claudio can now marry the pregnant Juliet. Angelo is punished by being forced to marry Mariana. Now the duke can declare his love for the chaste Isabella.

There are issues of justice and mercy, morality and the law, and sin and grace in this play. It is possible that Shakespeare began writing the play in leisure and was forced to finish it in haste.

> '*Man, proud man,*
> *Drest in a little brief authority,*
> *Most ignorant of what he's assur'd,*
> *His glassy essence, like an angry ape,*
> *Plays such fantastic tricks before high heaven,*
> *As make the angels weep.*'

> '*If thou art rich, thou'rt poor;*
> *For, like an ass whose back with ingots bows,*
> *Thou bear'st thy heavy riches but a journey,*
> *And death unloads thee.*'

> '*O! death's a great disguiser!*'

MUCH ADO ABOUT NOTHING

Written and performed in 1598-99

The chief sources are a novella by Bandello and an episode from Ariosto's '*Orlando Furioso*'. A popular comedy. The Prince of Aragon visits Leonato, the Duke of Messina, accompanied by Claudio and Benedick, the latter a sworn bachelor.

Leonato is the father of Hero and the uncle of Beatrice. Beatrice is a sprightly miss and has a teasing relationship with Benedick. They are tricked into believing they are in love which brings about an understanding between them.

Claudio is to marry Hero, but Don John, a malcontent brother of the prince, thwarts Claudio's marriage by arranging for him to see Hero being wooed on the balcony by his friend Borachio. It's her maidservant, Margaret, in disguise.

The plot devised by Don John and Borachio is unmasked by the 'shallow fools', Dogberry and Verges, the local constables.

As an amusing sequence Claudio promises to make amends to Leonato for his daughter's death, and is invited to marry Hero's cousin. Benedick asks to marry Beatrice at the same time and Hero's cousin turns out to be Hero herself.

So the play ends with a dance and with happy marriages.

> '*Sigh no more, ladies, sigh no more,*
> *Men were deceivers ever,*
> *One foot in the sea and one on shore,*
> *To one thing constant never.*'
>
> Balthasar

William Congreve (1670-1729) provided a further example of such happy marriages in '*The Way of the World*' with Millamant and Mirabell.

OTHELLO, THE MOOR OF VENICE

Written and performed in 1604-05. The source is a story in the *'Hecatommithi'* by Cinthio.

Othello is a Moor, a trusted general of the Venetian army. He has secretly married Desdemona, daughter of a senator, Brabantio. The audience quickly understands that Othello's ensign, Iago, is scheming against him for reasons which include the fact that Othello has chosen Michael Cassio as his lieutenant in preference to Iago.

Othello believes Iago to be utterly trustworthy, loyal and 'honest', yet it is at Iago's prompting that Roderigo, a foolish suitor for Desdemona's hand, reports the marriage to Brabantio.

Desdemona's father demands Othello's arrest, but accepts Desdemona's whole-hearted love for Othello when she has to appear before the senate.

The Turks are planning an attack on Cyprus, so that Othello has to leave immediately, and he is joined in Cyprus by Desdemona, Iago, Cassio and Roderigo.

The stage is therefore set for the treachery and tragedy which follow. The defeat of the Turkish army by Othello makes it possible for Iago to pursue his schemes in Cyprus. He manages to discredit Cassio so that Othello dismisses him.

Iago goes further, of course. He suggests to Cassio that he should appeal to Desdemona and at the same time implies to Othello that Cassio is more than friendly with Desdemona.

With Desdemona supporting Cassio, and with Iago's continuous innuendo, Othello soon becomes confused and suspicious. Desdemona accidentally drops a handkerchief given to her by Othello as the first token of his love. Iago finds it.

He hides it in Cassio's possessions and poor Cassio gives it to his mistress, Bianca. Othello sees the handkerchief in Bianca's possession which convinces him of Desdemona's infidelity. He humiliates her in public.

Then Iago incites Roderigo to kill Cassio, but Roderigo only wounds him, and Iago has to kill Roderigo to ensure his silence.

In a famous bedroom scene Othello kills Desdemona, overwhelmed by his belief in a tarnished love.

Emilia, Iago's wife, has been troubled by Iago's actions for some time, and reveals the truth to Venetian emissaries. Iago kills her, and is wounded by Othello but escapes.

Othello, remorseful, and having killed his beloved wife, has no other course but to kill himself. Iago is recaptured, tortured and imprisoned and Cassio is appointed to take command in Cyprus.

In '*Othello*', Shakespeare was able to present to an audience the conflict between the passionate but loyal Othello, rhetorically expressed, and the scheming Iago whose malice seems without explanation.

Choosing actors for these two parts has always been a casting problem.

> *'Put out the light, and then put out the light:*
> *If I quench thee, thou flaming minister,*
> *I can again thy former light restore,*
> *Should I repent me; but once put out thy light,*
> *Thou cunning'st pattern of excelling nature,*
> *I know not where is that Promethean heat*
> *That can thy light relume. When I have pluck'd thy rose*
> *I cannot give it vital growth again.'*
>
> Othello

YOU DEVIL, IAGO . . . !

'The devil's most devilish when respectable', wrote Elizabeth Barrett Browning (1806-1861). 'Get thee behind me, Satan', quoted St. Matthew.

Clever Iagos can usually undermine innocent Othellos. Imagine the conflict behind the curtain, when both Iago and Othello prepared for their stint on the stage.

Did they (do they now) sup afterwards with a pint of ale and a wry grin?

PERICLES, PRINCE OF TYRE

Written in 1607-08 and performed in 1608-09.

Shakespeare was 43 when this play was written and was to die only a few years later. It is believed that the first two Acts were written with a collaborator. The play is based on the story of Apollonius of Tyre in Gower's *'Confessio Amantis'*.

Gower, acting as Chorus, presents the play throughout.

He tells how Pericles, Prince of Tyre, finds his life in danger because he has discovered an incestuous relationship between King Antiochus and his daughter. He leaves his government in the control of Helicanus, his honest minister, and sails to Tarsus where he relieves a famine.

His ship is wrecked off the coast of Pentapolis and only Pericles survives. In a tournament he defeats suitors for the hand of Thaisa, daughter of King Simonides. Thaisa and Pericles marry.

When Pericles hears that Antiochus has died he sails to Tyre with Thaisa. During a storm Thaisa gives birth to Marina, a daughter, and faints. She is apparently dead, and is buried at sea in a chest. She is cast ashore at Ephesus. There, Cerimon, a physician, opens the chest and restores Thaisa to life. Thaisa believes her husband dead and becomes a priestess in the Temple of Diana.

Meanwhile Pericles takes Marina, his daughter, to Tarsus, where he leaves her with the Governor, Cleon, and his wife, Dyonyza. Dyonyza becomes jealous of Marina when she grows up, because she is more favoured than her own daughter, and she tries to kill her. Marina is carried off by pirates and sold in Mytilene to a brothel.

Her purity and piety win the admiration of the governor of the city, Lysimachus, and also the respect of the brothel-keeper's servant, Boult. She is released.

Pericles has a vision in which he is shown Marina's tomb, erected deceivingly by Cleon and Dyonyza. He sails for Mytilene where he discovers his daughter.

Then in a second vision, Diana directs him to her temple at Ephesus where he recounts the story of his life. Thaisa, the priestess, recognises him, and is reunited with husband and daughter, and at the end of the play the Chorus tells how Cleon and Dyonyza are burnt by citizens of Tarsus for their wickedness.

Third Fisherman: *Master, I marvel how the fishes live in the sea.*
First Fisherman: *Why, as men do a-land: the great ones eat up the little ones.*

IT WAS THE JOINER WHO DID IT

Imagine acting in Shoreditch without a theatre!

James Burbage, a joiner by trade, was also an actor.

He was born c1530 and was one of the Earl of Leicester's players in 1572. He was already 42 years of age, and used his ability as a joiner and his talent as an actor to lease land in Shoreditch in 1576 and erect, in wood, the first building intended for the presentation of plays.

In 1596 he acquired a house in Blackfriars and converted it into the Blackfriars Theatre. That was demolished in 1655 because of local opposition. The first English playhouse is mentioned in an Order of Council, dated August 1577. It was known as 'The Theatre'.

In December 1598 the fabric was removed to the Bankside and was set up as The Globe Theatre. So the Globe Theatre was erected in 1599 with materials from the old Theatre on the north side of the river.

It was a large, circular, thatched building with the centre open to the sky. The thatch caught fire in 1613, owing to the discharge of guns as the king entered in the play Henry VIII.

The whole building was destroyed, and was rebuilt in 1614. It was demolished in 1644.

Shakespeare had gone to London to seek fortune on the London stage at the age of 20. it was 1584. The close connection between James Burbage and Richard Burbage (his son) developed from the time of Shakespeare's arrival in London, and his impact on the London stage.

Shakespeare was a provincial. He had left his wife, Anne, with three children in Stratford-upon-Avon, in a desperate attempt to use his talents in the capital city.

When Shakespeare and Richard Burbage met they were very much of a similar age, and the brilliant, provincial young man found in Richard Burbage a Londoner who could act in his plays. Richard Burbage, the joiner's son, rose to be an actor of chief parts, excelling in tragedy and appearing in plays by Jonson and Beaumont and Fletcher, quite apart from Shakespeare's plays.

So Shakespeare, the provincial, linked with Burbage, the Londoner, and was able to be accepted as a sharer in the theatres which grew from their association. What a remarkable coincidence!

Imagine the almost-feverish outpourings of Shakespeare at this time.

There were packed houses at the theatres. No TV, no radio, No Sky-TV, no diversion other than Richard Burbage, Edward Alleyne, and Will Kempe, and Shakespeare appearing in odd parts while probably scribbling off-stage fresh lines for the actors and developing the structure of a new play.

Thank you, James Burbage. You built the Blackfriars Theatre. Shakespeare acted there and later had a share. A just reward for this great man of British literature. And, of course, for all joiners!

RICHARD II

Written and performed in 1595. The main source is Holinshed's *'Chronicles'*. This is an historical tragedy, dealing with the deposition of an anointed king.

The play opens with a conflict between two great noblemen, Thomas Morbay, Duke of Norfolk, and Henry Bolingbroke, Earl of Hereford.

Richard II requires them to settle their differences in a duel at Coventry. Suddenly, when all the preparations hae been made, the king interrupts the proceedings and banishes them both.

When John of Gaunt, Bolingbroke's father, dies, Richard confiscates Bolingbroke's inheritance because he needs the money to finance his Irish wars.

This gives Bolingbroke a reason for returning from exile with an invading force. He gains the support of many English lords who have been over-taxed by Richard II, and is encouraged to claim the throne.

In a famous scene Richard II stages his own deposition. He is confined to Pomfret castle, where he has time to reflect on the divine right of kings.

Bolingbroke is threatened by conspiracies and exercises diplomacy and discipline, showing kingly qualities superior to those of Richard II. At Pomfret, Richard II is killed by Sir Pierce of Exton, although Bolingbroke repudiates him later. As an expiation for this obvious regicide Bolingbroke, now Henry IV, expresses his intention to make a pilgrimage to the Holy Land.

Apparently Shakespeare's company earned Queen Elizabeth's displeasure by performing the play on the eve of the Earl of Essex's rebellion in 1601.

> '. . . Exton, thy fierce hand
> Hath with the king's blood stained the king's own land;
> Mount, mount, my soul, thy seat is up on high,
> Whilst my gross flesh sinks downward, here to die.'

Richard II

THIS SCEPTRED ISLE

'This royal throne of kings, this sceptred isle,
This earth of majesty, this seat of Mars,
This other Eden, demi-paradise,
This fortress built by nature for herself
Against infection and the hand of war,
This happy breed of men, this little world,
This precious stone set in a silver sea,
Which serves it in the office of a wall,
Or as a moat defensive to a house,
Against the envy of less happier lands;
This blessed plot, this earth, this realm, this England,
This nurse, this teeming womb of royal kings,
Fear'd by their breed, and famous by their birth.
Renowned for their deeds as far from home, –
For Christian service and true chivalry, –
As is the sepulchre in stubborn Jewry
Of the world's ransom, blessed Mary's Son:
This land of such dear souls, this dear, dear land,
Dear for her reputation through the world,
Is now leas'd out, – I die pronouncing it, –
Like to a tenement or pelting farm:
England, bound in with the triumphant sea,
Whose rocky shore beats back the envious siege
Of watery Neptune, is now bound in with shame,
With inky blots, and rotten parchment bonds:
That England, that was wont to conquer others,
Hath made a shameful conquest of itself.'

John of Gaunt

RICHARD III

Written and performed in 1592-93.

The chief sources are Holinshed's *'Chronicles',* material from Vergil's *'Anglicae Historiae',* and Sir Thomas More's *'The History of King Richard the Thirde'.*

This play completes the tetralogy (four related literary works) of which the first three parts are *Henry VI Part I, Henry VI Part II* and *Henry VI Part III.*

Richard of Gloucester, who becomes Richard III, is deformed. He is ambitious, brave, bloody, bold, murderous, subtle, treacherous and a usurper of the crown of England. He is determined to become king and sets out to destroy all opposition.

First, he ensures that his brother, the Duke of Clarence, imprisoned in the Tower of London, is murdered. He woos Anne as she accompanies the corpse of her father-in-law, Henry VI, to his grave. Later he marries her.

He attacks Queen Elizabeth's family and supporters, with the help of the Duke of Buckingham. Hastings, Rivers and Grey are all executed, and Richard is proclaimed King of England because Buckingham has persuaded the citizens of London. When crowned, Richard arranges the murder of his nephews (the Princes in the Tower).

Anne, his wife, dies, and he attempts to marry his niece, Elizabeth of York. But the Duke of Buckingham rebels and joins Henry Tudor, Earl of Richmond. The Earl has landed at Milford Haven in Wales to claim the crown. Buckingham is captured and executed, but now Richard has to face Richmond's army at Bosworth.

On the night before the battle ghosts appear to Richard. They are the ghosts of those whom Richard has murdered or has had murdered and they have appeared to foretell of his defeat. They do.

Richard loses his horse in the battle, and is killed by Richmond, who then becomes Henry VII, the first of the Tudor monarchs.

Richard III is, of course, a great acting role, and has been acted by great actors – including Laurence Olivier.

> *'My conscience hath a thousand several tongues,*
> *And every tongue brings in a several tale,*
> *And every tale condemns me for a villain.'*
>
> Richard III

NEVER FORGET THE ACTORS

Playwrights write plays. Theatre impresarios back them. Producers direct them. Stage-managers arrange them. And .... **actors perform them.**

Never forget the actor, for it is he or she who, because of a special histrionic talent, make the playwright, the impresario, the producer and the stage-manager benefit from the playwright's first idea.

Shakespeare dreamt of the plays from his vast reading when he arrived in London in 1584. Little is known of his struggle as a young man of 20, with three tiny children left in Stratford-upon-Avon, entirely dependent upon his father, knowing instinctively that he could make a living for himself and his family on the London stage.

Meeting James Burbage, the joiner/actor, Richard Burbage, Edward Alleyne and Will Kempe in the London theatrical scene produced from Shakespeare the greatness he must have inherited.

It was those actors who were able to present his plays and his characters to the public. Other great Shakespearean actors have followed, but none so great as Laurence Olivier.

Shakespeare was himself an actor, and therefore knew that his words, his poetry, his dramatic verse could only be best presented by a great actor. He was fortunate to meet Burbage and Alleyne. Had he met Olivier he would have been even more fortunate.

> 'As in a theatre, the eyes of men,
> After a well-grac'd actor leaves the stage,
> Are idly bent on him that enters next,
> Thinking his prattle to be tedious;
> Even so, and with much more contempt, men's eyes
> Did scowl on Richard.'
> So wrote Shakespeare in his *Richard III*.

And so acted Laurence Olivier as the hunchback Richard III in London's theatreland after World War II. Olivier produced, acted and played in films of *Henry V, Hamlet, Richard III, Othello*. His Titus was 'memorable'.

Great actors aspire to play great parts. Shakespeare wrote great parts, and great comedians have often aspired to play great Shakespearian tragedic characters. Only the actors can perpetuate the playwright's plan.

Shakespeare's plays are so numerous, so universally accepted, that their perpetuation can only be achieved on the stage itself, where the personality of the actor, projecting the character created by Shakespeare, can delight a live audience.

Imagine the Proms without a live audience! This is why theatres where Shakespeare's plays are presented to a live audience are now growing throughout the world, and why the Globe Theatre is once again opening for the public.

Come back, you actors! Shakespeare. Burbage. Alleyne. Olivier. Share a box!

ROMEO AND JULIET

Written 1591-96 and performed 1594-95. The source was well known.

Verona is blighted by the feud between two great families – the Capulets and the Montagues. There is a street brawl, and the Prince of Verona orders both families to keep the peace on pain of death.

Capulet plans a masqued ball to announce the marriage of his daughter, Juliet, to Count Paris. Romeo, Montague's love-sick son, attends to find Rosalind whom he loves. He meets Juliet and they fall in love immediately.

Tybalt recognises him and wants to fight him.

Romeo waits under Juliet's balcony and plans a secret marriage, assisted by Juliet's nurse and their mutual confessor, Friar Lawrence.

After the marriage Romeo attempts to stop a duel between his friend Mercutio and Tybalt. Mercutio is killed and Romeo kills Tybalt. He is banished from Verona after a single night with his new wife.

Friar Lawrence plans to make the secret marriage public, but before he can do so Capulet decides that Juliet must marry Count Paris immediately.

The Friar advises her to acquiesce, but gives her a potion to take just before the wedding. He tells her the potion will give her the appearance of death which will last for 48 hours. Then he will arrange for her to be taken to the family vault, where the Friar will arrange for Romeo to greet her when she awakes.

Friar Lawrence's message fails to reach Romeo because of plague. Romeo is desperate when he hears of Juliet's death and buys poison. He visits the Capulet vault for a last sight of Juliet and, finding Count Paris there, kills him. He then drinks the poison and dies. Juliet wakes, sees Romeo dead and stabs herself with his dagger.

This sequence is related by Friar Lawrence at the end of the play, and the result is a reconciliation of the two families, the play ending with some measure of relief.

Shakespeare's virtuosity is indicated here, for at the same time he was writing the *'Pyramid and Thisbe'* play in *Midsummer Night's Dream*. He reached lyrical heights with his love poetry, so that despite over-familiarity the play is always popular.

> *'Good night, good night! Parting is such sweet sorrow*
> *That I shall say good night till it be morrow.'*
>
> Juliet

ARE <u>YOU</u> IN LOVE?

Tongue-tied? Smitten by her beauty? Staggered by her intellect? Overcome with youthful desire?
Imagine you're Romeo and your girlfriend is Juliet, and rehearse the following lines:

You:	Lady, by yonder blessed moon I swear
	That tips with silver all these fruit-tree tops,
Your girlfriend:	O! swear not by the moon, the inconstant moon,
	That monthly changes in her circled orb,
	Lest that thy love prove likewise variable.
You:	What shall I swear by?
Your girlfriend:	Do not swear at all,
	Or, if thou wilt, swear by thy gracious self,
	Which is the god of my idolatry.

That will do the trick. 'WS' knew all the answers, and you'll find even more to woo your girlfriend in the sonnets that follow.

THE COMEDY OF ERRORS

Written in 1591, performed in 1592-93. Acted at Gray's Inn in 1594.

A comedy by Shakespeare signifies a play which is not a tragedy, and therefore a comedy has a happy ending whatever may take place during the action.

Syracuse and Ephesus are enemies. If a Syracusan is found in Ephesus he is put to death unless he pays 1,000 marks as ransom.

Egeon, who is an old Syracusan merchant, has been arrested in Ephesus. On the duke's orders he has to explain how he came to be there. He explains that he and his wife Emilia had twin sons, exactly alike, and both named Antipholus. They purchased twin slaves, each named Dromio, to attend on their sons.

They had all become separated in a shipwreck, so that Egeon was left with his younger one and one slave, whilst his wife was left with the other son and the other slave. Egeon had not seen his wife, son or slave since.

The younger son, Antipholus of Syracuse, on reaching manhood, had gone in search of his mother and twin brother, accompanied by his slave, Dromio. That was five years ago, and Egeon had sought him all over the world, finally arriving in Ephesus.

The duke is deeply affected by this tale and gives Egeon till the evening to find the 1,000 marks ransom. As it happens, the elder Antipholus (of Ephesus), with his Dromio, has been living in Ephesus since the shipwreck. He is also married.

And, as it also happens, Antipholus of Syracuse and his Dromio have arrived at Ephesus that very morning. And the twins still resemble each other perfectly! The comedy of errors results from this setting.

Antipholus of Syracuse is summoned to dinner by Dromio of Ephesus. He is claimed as husband by the wife of Antipholus of Ephesus, the latter being refused admittance to his own house. Why? Because he is already believed to be within. And Antipholus of Syracuse (he's the unmarried one) falls in love with Luciana, his brother's wife's sister.

Finally, Antipholus of Ephesus is confined as a lunatic, and Antipholus of Syracuse hides from his brother's jealous wife in a convent.

It is now evening, and Egeon is about to be executed. As the duke makes his way to the place of execution, Antipholus of Ephesus appeals to him for clemency. Then the Abbess of the convent presents Antipholus of Syracuse, who is also claiming clemency.

The appearance of two identical twins is sufficient to explain the many misunderstandings, and Egeon recovers his two sons and his liberty.

You must have guessed. The Abbess is the lost wife, Emilia!

> *'They brought one Pinch, a hungry lean-fac'd villain,*
> *A mere anatomy, a mountebank,*
> *A threadbare juggler, and a fortune-teller,*
> *A needy, hollow-ey'd, sharp-looking wretch,*
> *A living dead man.'*
>
> Antipholus of Ephesus

JAMES I LIKED IT

Even in 1604 this play was in demand at James I's court, and was in the repertoire of The King's Men for many years. The King's Men was the finest of Elizabethan theatre companies, and enjoyed James I's personal patronage.

The shareholders were Burbage, Phillips, Heminges and Shakespeare. The repertoire included works by Jonson, Webster, Tourneur, Middleton, Marston, Beaumont and Fletcher.

In 1608 they added the indoor Blackfriars to the outdoor Globe, and performed at both. Theatres were closed in 1642 under the Puritans, and it was not until 1662, at Drury Lane, that the company re-assembled under the patronage of Charles II.

THE MERCHANT OF VENICE

Written and performed 1596-98.

The main source was a story by Giovanni Fiorentino. Shakespeare perhaps knew of Marlowe's *'The Jew of Malta'* which was first produced in 1590.

Antonio, a Venetian merchant, is awaiting the return of his ships. He is asked for a loan by his friend Bassanio, who wishes to marry Portia, heiress of Belmont.

Until his ship's return, Antonio is without money and borrows from Shylock, a Jewish moneylender. Shylock hates Antonio for his generosity because it reduces the rate of usury in Venice. Shylock agrees to make the loan without interest, but with the forfeit of a pound of Antonio's flesh as a bond.

Bassanio succeeds in winning Portia's hand because he chooses the right casket in a test in Portia's father's will. They are about to celebrate their marriage when news is received of the foundering of Antonio's ships.

Shylock has demanded his pound of flesh, and the case is to be tried before the Duke of Venice. The setting is made more acrimonious because his daughter, Jessica, has eloped with Lorenzo, a friend of Bassanio.

Antonio is represented in court by an unknown advocate and clerk (Portia and her maid Nerissa in male disguises) but Shylock rejects Portia's famous plea for mercy and demands the bond. Portia, however, points out that the bond is for flesh only and that no blood must be spilled.

The Duke upholds the point, and Shylock is defeated. He is pardoned, provided he gives half his wealth to Antonio and becomes a Christian.

There are celebrations during which Portia and Nerissa reveal their true identities, and at the same time news is received that Antonio's ships have arrived safely after all.

The character of Shylock has obvious theatrical impact, and until 1880 the play ended with his final exit.

'The quality of mercy is not strain'd,
It droppeth as the gentle rain from heaven
Upon the place beneath: It is twice blest;
It blesseth him that gives and him that takes:
'Tis mightiest in the mightiest: it becomes
The throned monarch better than his crown;
His sceptre shows the force of temporal power,
The attribute to awe and majesty,
Wherein doth sit the dread and fear of kings;
But mercy is above this sceptred sway,
It is enthroned in the hearts of kings,
It is an attribute to God himself,
And earthly power doth then show likest God's
When mercy seasons justice.'

Portia

Lorenzo to Jessica:

'How sweet the moonlight sleeps upon this bank!
Here will we sit, and let the sounds of music
Creep in our ears; soft stillness and the night
Become the sweet touches of harmony.
Sit, Jessica: look, how the floor of heaven
Is thick inlaid with patines of bright gold:
There's not the smallest orb which thou behold'st
But in his motion like an angel sings
Still quiring to the young-eyed cherubins;
Such harmony is in immortal souls;
But, whilst this muddy vesture of decay
Doth grossly close it in, we cannot hear it.'

**Try that on your girlfriend and she'll swoon at
your feet!**

THE MERRY WIVES OF WINDSOR

Written in 1597 and performed 1600.

The play may have been written for the occasion of the installation as a Knight of the Garter of George Carey, Lord Hunsdon, on 23 April, 1597. It was probably also written in response to public demand because of the great stage character, Falstaff.

Falstaff is in 'financial difficulties'. He decides to make love to the wives of Ford and Page, two gentlemen who live at Windsor, because they control the purses of their husbands. But Nym and Pistol, who have been discarded by Falstaff, warn the husbands, and when Falstaff sends identical love-letters to Mrs. Ford and Mrs. Page the wives arrange the Knight's discomfiture.

When the first assignation takes place, at Ford's house, they hide Falstaff in a basket, cover him with foul linen and have him tipped into a muddy ditch.

At the next assignation they disguise him as the 'fat woman of Brainford', in which character he is chastised by Ford. Now the assignation is made in Windsor Forest, where Falstaff is beaten and pinched by mock fairies and is then exposed by Ford and Page.

There is a sub-plot. Anne, the daughter of Page, is pursued by three suitors: Doctor Caius, a French physician, Slender, the foolish cousin of Justice Swallow, and Fenton, a wild young gentleman, whom Anne really loves. Mistress Quickly is the servant to Dr. Caius and acts as impartial go-between for all three suitors.

Sir Hugh Evans, a Welsh parson, interferes and there is an altercation with the irascible Dr. Caius.

When the final assignation has been made, Page (who favours Slender for his daughter) arranges for her to be carried off in white. Mrs. Page, who favours Dr. Caius, arranges that she shall be carried off in green. Both of them are fobbed off with a boy in disguise.

Fenton, the wild one, has run off with Anne and married her! Great fun for all except for Falstaff and the thwarted lovers.

> *'O, what a world of vile ill-favoured faults*
> *Looks handsome in three hundred pounds a year!'*
>
> Anne Page

THE TAMING OF THE SHREW

Written in 1593 and performed in 1593-94

The source of the main plot is George Gascoigne's *'Supposes'*, a translation from Ariosto or, it is supposed, from an earlier lost play.

The introduction to the play is through the medium of a lord who plays a practical joke on a drunken tinker, Christopher Sly, inviting him to witness a comedy being presented by a group of travelling players.

Baptista is a rich Paduan. He will not allow his younger daughter, Bianca, to be married until a husband has been found for her sister, Katharina. But nobody wants Katharina, for she is notoriously ill-tempered.

Petruchio is a visitor from Verona who is in search of a rich wife, and decides to take her on.

Ignoring her rudeness, and accepting good-naturedly what others find offensive, he manages to organise the marriage. Once arranged, he begins his systematic taming of the shrew.

He arrives late at the wedding, wearing rags and riding an old horse. And he rushes Katharina off before the wedding feast. Then he embarks on a programme of humiliation which finally subdues Katharina.

When Petruchio returns to Baptista's house he is able to present Katharina as the most docile wife in the whole company.

In the interim Bianca has married Lucentio and is not as docile as Katharina now is.

A good comedy play.

Was it sparked off by some trifling domestic contretemps Shakespeare endured in his own domain at Stratford? Who will ever know?

> *'Our purses shall be proud, our garments poor;*
> *For 'tis the mind that makes the body rich;*
> *And as the sun breaks through the darkest clouds,*
> *So honour peereth in the meanest habit.'*

Petruchio

THE TEMPEST

Written in 1611 and performed 1611-12. Regarded as Shakespeare's last play, and performed before the king in Whitehall.

It was also included in the wedding celebrations for the Princess Elizabeth and the Elector of Palestine.

Shakespeare wrote the play without any collaborator before retiring to Stratford.

Dr. Samuel Johnson considered the plan of the play 'regular', i.e. conforming to the three unities of action, time and space.

Prospero, the Duke of Milan, has been ousted from his throne by his brother, Antonio, and turned adrift in a boat with his child, Miranda. They are ship-wrecked upon a lonely island. As a coincidence Sycorax, the witch, had been banished to the same island.

Prospero has a knowledge of magic and has therefore released various spirits, including Ariel, who have been imprisoned by the witch. They now obey his orders.

The sole inhabitant of the island is Caliban, a mis-shapen monster, who is the witch's son, and Prospero has also engaged him in service. In this way Prospero and Miranda have survived on the island for twelve years.

The play begins with a shipwreck, engineered by Prospero, so that Antonio, his confederate Alonso (the King of Naples), his brother Sebastian and his son, Ferdinand, now find themselves on the same island. All the passengers are saved, but Ferdinand is presumed drowned and he himself presumes the others are drowned.

Prospero's plan is for Miranda and Ferdinand to fall in love and to become engaged. On another part of the island Sebastian and Antonio are plotting to kill Alonso and Gonzalo, who had helped Prospero in his banishment.

Caliban offers his services to Stephano, a drunken butler, and to Trinculo, the court jester, and persuades Sebastian and Antonio to try to murder Prospero. As the conspirators draw near, Prospero breaks off the masque of Iris, Juno and Ceres, which Ariel is presenting to Ferdinand and Miranda to celebrate the plighting of their troths.

Caliban, Stephano, and Trinculo are driven away and Ariel brings the king and his courtiers, together with Gonzalo, to Prospero.

Prospero is now able to greet Gonzalo, his 'true preserver', and to forgive Antonio on condition that he restores Prospero's kingdom to him. He is also able to reunite Alonso with his son, Ferdinand.

Alonso repents, and Antonio and Sebastian accept their new situation. Miraculously, the boatswain and the master of the ship appear to say that the ship is repaired and the crew is safe.

So all embark for Italy, Prospero releases Ariel from his service, and renounces his magic.

Only Caliban, the naughty monster, is left alone on the island.

There have been many literary works based upon *'The Tempest'*: Milton's *'Comus'*, Browning's *'Caliban upon Setebos'*, Shelley's *'Ariel and Miranda'*, and a series of poetic meditations by W.H.Auden, entitled *'The Sea and The Mirror'*.

There is also an excellent science fiction film *'Forbidden Planet'* (1954).

> *'Full fathom five thy father lies;*
> *Of his bones are coral made;*
> *Those are pearls that were his eyes;*
> *Nothing of him that doth fade*
> *But doth suffer a sea-change*
> *Into something rich and strange.'*

Ariel

John Milton (1608-1674) was born when Shakespeare was 44, so he was only 8 when Shakespeare died.

His 'Comus' was presented at Ludlow Castle in 1634. Its theme, the confrontation between evil and virtue is serious and always recurrent in Milton's poetry, and its relationship with *'The Tempest'* is tenuous.

Caliban was presumably the 'evil', and the final happy outcome was the 'virtue'.

TWO GENTLEMEN OF VERONA

zWritten in 1590 and performed in 1594

The source is a story by Jorge de Montemayor called *'Diana Enoramada'*. A play acted at court, now lost, may also have been a source. It was called *'The History of Felix and Philiomena'*.

Valentine leaves Verona and his friend Proteus and goes to Milan. He meets the Duke's daughter Silvia and falls in love with her but the Duke wants her to marry the foolish Thurio.

Proteus arrives in Milan, having been sent by his father. Before he leaves he exchanges rings as tokens of love for Julia, from whom he takes a solemn farewell.

He is welcomed by Valentine and Silvia, but falls in love with Silvia and tells the Duke of the couple's intention to elope. As a result Valentine is banished to Milan.

Julia has followed Proteus disguised as a boy and she enters his service without being recognised. To her dismay she is given her ring by Proteus, and is sent to Silvia with it to express his love.

Silvia wants neither Proteus nor Thurio, and she runs away to find Valentine. She is captured by robbers. She is not aware that Valentine has become the leader of a band of 'honourable outlaws'.

Proteus rescues Silvia, and Valentine observes her former friend's attempts to win Silvia for himself. When Proteus asks Valentine to forgive him Julia faints, revealing the ring Proteus gave her in Milan.

The couples are reconciled, of course, and as the Duke of Milan is now prepared to accept Valentine as a more suitable suitor for his daughter, they all return to Milan for a double wedding and the usual celebrations.

The part of Proteus's servant, Launce, was probably written for Will Kempe, who was famous as a clown in the Elizabethan theatre. Kempe was a member of the Lord Chamberlain's company when it was decided to build the Globe on the South Bank in 1597-98. He played Peter in *'Romeo and Juliet'* and Dogberry in *'Much Ado About Nothing'*.

> *'Who is Silvia? what is she,*
> *That all our swains commend her?*
> *Holy, fair, and wise is she;*
> *The heaven such grace did lend her,*
> *That she might admired be.'*
>
> A Song in the Play

THE WINTER'S TALE

Written and performed in 1610-11. The main source is Robert Green's romance *'Pandosto'* (1588)

Leontes, King of Sicily, has entertained his childhood friend, Polixenes, King of Bohemia, for several months. He is suddenly obsessed with an insane jealousy by the closeness of the friendship between his queen, Hermione, and Polixenes, and instructs his adviser Camillo to poison the latter. But Camillo warns Polixenes and escapes with him to Bohemia. Leontes imprisons his pregnant wife and charges her with adultery and a conspiracy to poison him.

The Delphic oracle pronounces Hermione to be chaste and Leontes a 'jealous tyrant', but he defies its message. His daughter has been carried off by Antigonus, although only recently born.

Then comes news of the death of Leontes' son and a report that Hermione has also died. The report is from Antigonus' outraged wife. Leontes is shamed, and vows to spend the rest of his life in penance.

Meanwhile Antigonus has taken the innocent child to the Bohemian shore, leaving her there with a store of gold and naming her 'Perdita'. Antigonus is eaten by a bear and an old shepherd finds Perdita.

There is a sixteen year gap, which is explained by Time as Chorus, and the second part of the play begins, intended to be a comedy of rebirth and renewal. Perdita has been brought up in a humble shepherd's home, and yet she has attracted the love of Polixenes' son, Prince Florizel. But Polixenes comes in disguise to attend the sheep-shearing ceremony and shatters everyone by demanding the end of the match.

Perdita and Florizel escape to Sicily, with Camillo's help, and there they are welcomed by Leontes. The vengeful Polixenes has followed them and, with all the others, learns of Perdita's true birth. He welcomes the marriage as a mark of reconciliation with Leontes.

Pauline, the wife of Antigonus, gathers all the leading characters to see the newly-completed statue of Hermione, and as Leontes looks at it with wonder Pauline calls for music. The statue comes to life! Hermione is 'reborn' into her marriage with Leontes.

The play is a romance with many facets and was first performed at the Blackfriars, where John Fletcher's works were popular.

> *'What you do*
> *Still better what is done. When you speak, sweet,*
> *I'd have you do it ever. When you sing,*
> *I'd have you buy and sell so; so give alms;*
> *Pray so; and, for the ord'ring your affairs,*
> *To sing them too.'*
>
> Florizel

TIMON OF ATHENS

Written in 1605-09 and performed 1607-08.

The story may have been read by Shakespeare in Plutarch's *'Life of Mark Antony'*.

Timon is a rich, noble Athenian whose generosity leaves him impoverished. He asks his rich friends for help but finds that those who previously sought his company now avoid him.

He arranges a banquet for them, and throws bowls of water in their faces in disgust. Then he leaves Athens, followed only by his faithful servant, Flavius.

Timon is now a misanthrope. He lives in a cave, digging for roots, and uncovers a hoard of gold. When he is visited by the exiled Athenian general, Alcibiades, who is on the way to Athens with an avenging army, Timon gives him gold to pay his soldiers.

He gives the remains of his treasure to Flavius for his loyalty, and swears him to silence. Apemantus, a philosopher, spreads news of Timon's sudden riches, and the Athenian senators come to him for help against Alcibiades.

Timon refuses, and Alcibiades is victorious.

The victor promises to destroy only those who are his or Timon's enemies, but on hearing of Timon's death he is magnanimous and offers peace with mercy.

> *'Tis not enough to help the feeble up,*
> *But to support him after.'*

Timon

The Chibchas were South American Indians of Colombis who had a practice of covering their chief with gold dust, after applying an underlay of gum, thus fostering the name of El Dorado, the city of gold.

Timon discovered his own El Dorado!

STRATFORD-UPON-AVON

A market town in Warwickshire to which millions of people come from all over the world to see where William Shakespeare was born.

He was the eldest son of John, a glover and wool dealer. Traditionally, his birthday is celebrated on St. George's Day, 23rd April. The register of Holy Trinity Church, Stratford, records that he was christened there on 26th April, 1564, and died at his home in Stratford on 23rd April, 1616.

He had lodgings in London and used most of his very considerable income to increase the security and status of his family in their Stratford home, spending time with them between theatre seasons. When he was in his late forties he left London to spend the remainder of his life in Stratford.

Stratford-upon-Avon is now one of the most important tourist centres of Britain, through the heritage of Shakespeare.

On 28th November 1582, a bond was issued permitting him to marry Anne Hathaway of Shottery, a village close to Stratford. He was 18 and she was 8 years his senior. A daughter, Susanna, was baptized on 26th May, 1583 and twins (Hamnet and Judith) on 2nd February 1585.

When Shakespeare made his theatrical and playwrighting career in London his family remained in Stratford. In 1596 his father applied successfully for a grant of arms, and so became a gentleman.

In August Hamnet died, and was buried in Holy Trinity churchyard.

In 1597 Shakespeare was able to purchase New Place, and his father died in 1601. In 1602 William paid £320 for 127 acres of land in Old Stratford, and in the next year paid £440 for an interest in the Stratford tythes.

In 1607 his daughter Susanna married a physician, John Hall. William's only granddaughter, Elizabeth Hall, was christened the following February, and in 1608 his mother died and was buried in Holy Trinity. In February 1616, Shakespeare's second daughter, Judith, married Thomas Quiney, causing him to make alterations to the draft of his will, which he signed on 25th March.

He died on 23rd April 1616, and was buried at Holy Trinity. His widow died in 1623 and his last surviving descendant, Elizabeth Hall, in 1670.

Rather like Hollywood scriptwriters, his plays were being written as they were performed. Records of performances are scanty and haphazard, and as a result dates and order of composition are difficult to establish. The dates are the subject of considerable study by scholars.

But as Jonsen wrote that 'Shakespeare was not of an age, but for all time' perhaps the plays themselves and his great dramatic poetry should be enough. The play scripts have been translated into innumerable languages and have inspired poets, novelists, dramatists, painters, composers, choreographers, film-makers and other artists at all levels of creative activity.

He was 'the Bard of Stratford-upon-Avon'.

TITUS ANDRONICUS

Written in 1589 and performed in 1593-94.

There are various sources, including Euripedes' *'Hecuba'*, Seneca's *'Thyestes'* and *'Troades'*, and Plutarch's *'Metamorphoses'*.

The play is in two halves. In the final half Titus returns to Rome after his sixth victory over the Goths. He brings with him Queen Tamora of the Goths and her three sons. The eldest, Alarbus, is sacrificed to avenge the deaths of his own sons.

Titus is offered the title of Emperor, but chooses the late Emperor's son Saturninus, who is to marry his own daughter, Lavinia.

But Saturninus' brother claims Lavinia for himself, and Titus is forced to kill a certain Mutius whilst Lavinia is being taken away.

Saturninus now changes his mind and renounces Lavinia. He marries Queen Tamora, who is engineering a false reconciliation between the Emperor and Titus. She plans to destroy the latter, with the help of her lover Aaron, the Moor, who arranges for her sons,Chiron and Demetrius, to murder Bassianus and throw his body into a pit.

Lavinia is raped, and her tongue and hands are cut off. Titus' sons, Quintus and Martius, are then lured by Aaron to fall into the pit, where they are found and accused of the murder of Bassianus. Aaron tells Titus that his sons will be spared if he, Titus, sacrifices his hand and sends it to the Emperor.

Titus does this, but it is returned with the heads of his two sons.

In the second half of the play, Titus discovers who raped and mutilated Lavinia, and with his brother, Marcus, and his remaining son, Lucius, he vows revenge. Lucius leaves Rome, to return with an amy of Goths. Aaron and his child by Tamora are captured.

Tamora and her sons, Demetrius and Chiron, visit Titus disguised as Revenge, Rapine and Murder, and ask him to have Lucius banquet at his house, to which the Emperor, the Empress and her sons will be brought.

Titus recognises his enemies and with the help of Lavinia he slits the throats of Chiron and Demetrius. He even uses their flesh in a pie, some of which Tamora eats at the banquet before Titus kills her. He also stabs Lavinia, and is then killed by Saturninus, who is in turn killed by Lucius.

Lucius is elected Emperor, and sentences Aaron to be buried breast-deep in the ground and starved to death.

Blood thirsty? It is probably Shakespeare's first tragedy, and has been praised as the forerunner of Shakespeare's great tragedies – 'Othello' and 'King Lear'.

A drawing of 'Tamora pleadinge for her sonnes going to execution' dated 1595 and ascribed to Henry Peacham, hangs at Longleat in Wiltshire.

> 'She is a woman, therefore may be woo'd;
> She is a woman, therefore may be won;
> She is Lavinia, therefore must be lov'd.
> What, man! more water glideth by the mill
> That wots the miller of; and easy it is
> Of a cut loaf to steal a shive, we know.'
>
> Demetrius

HE WAS ONLY TWENTY-THREE

Our hero is now in London.

His great rival, Christopher Marlowe, the son of a shoemaker, had won a scholarship at Cambridge. He had become an agent of Francis Walsingham, and was possibly in Elizabeth I's secret service.

Marlowe had taken his BA in 1584 (Shakespeare was then involved at Stratford with three tiny children) and his MA in 1587.

Almost immediately afterwards Marlowe had presented the London theatre with the startling success of Tamburlaine the Great, which was superbly delivered by Edward Alleyne, the leading performer of the Lord Admiral's Men.

Had Marlowe not been killed in a tavern brawl in 1593, would our hero have been so successful?

Come forward, Sherlock Holmes, Pierot, Columbo and Morse. Who killed Marlowe, so that William Shakespeare was able to produce those brilliant plays and emerge as Britain's great playwright?

SHAKESPEARE'S SONNETS

1

From fairest creatures we desire increase,
That thereby beauty's Rose might never die,
But as the riper should by time decease,
His tender heir might bear his memory:
But thou, contracted to thine own bright eyes,
Feed'st thy light's flame with self-substantial fuel,
Making a famine where abundance lies,
Thyself thy foe, to thy sweet self too cruel.
Thou that art now the world's fresh ornament,
And only herald to the gaudy spring,
Within thine own bud buriest thy content,
And, tender churl, makest waste in niggarding.
　　Pity the world, or else this glutton be,
　　To eat the world's due, by the grave and thee.

2

When forty winters shall besiege thy brow,
And dig deep trenches in thy beauty's field,
Thy youth's proud livery, so gazed on now,
Will be a totter'd weed, of small worth held:
Then being askt where all thy beauty lies,
Where all the treasure of thy lusty days;
To say, within thine own deep-sunken eyes,
Were an all-eating shame and thriftless praise.
How much more praise deserved thy beauty's use,
If thou couldst answer, 'This fair child of mine
Shall sum my count, and make my old excuse,'
Proving his beauty by succession thine!
　　This were to be new made when thou art old,
　　And see thy blood warm when thou feel'st it cold.

3

Look in thy glass, and tell the face thou viewest
Now is the time that face should form another;
Whose fresh repair if now thou not renewest.
Thou dost beguile the world, unbless some mother.
For where is she so fair whose unear'd womb
Disdains the tillage of thy husbandry?
Or who is he so fond will be the tomb
Of his self-love, to stop posterity?
Thou art thy mother's glass, and she in thee
Calls back the lovely April of her prime:
So thou through windows of thine age shalt see,
Despite of wrinkles, this thy golden time.
　　But if thou live, remember'd not to be,
　　Die single, and thine image dies with thee.

4

Unthrifty loveliness, why dost thou spend
Upon thyself thy beauty's legacy?
Nature's bequest gives nothing; but doth lend;
And, being frank, she lends to those are free.
Then, beauteous niggard, why dost thou abuse
The bounteous largess given thee to give?
Profitless usurer, why dost thou use
So great a sum of sums, yet canst not live?
For having traffic with thyself alone,
Thou of thyself thy sweet self dost deceive.
Then how, when nature calls thee to be gone,
What acceptable audit canst thou leave?
    Thy unused beauty must be tomb'd with thee,
    Which, used, lives th' executor to be.

5

Those hours, that with gentle work did frame
The lovely gaze where every eye doth dwell,
Will play the tyrants to the very same,
And that unfair which fairly doth excel:
For never-resting time leads summer on
To hideous winter and confounds him there;
Sap checkt with frost, and lusty leaves quite gone,
Beauty o'ersnow'd, and bareness every where:
Then, were not summer's distillation left,
A liquid prisoner pent in walls of glass,
Beauty's effect with beauty were bereft,
Nor it, nor no remembrance what it was:
    But flowers distill'd, though they with winter meet,
    Leese but their show; their substance still lives sweet.

6

Then let not winter's ragged hand deface
In thee thy summer, ere thou be distill'd:
Make sweet some vial; treasure thou some place
With beauty's treasure, ere it be self-kill'd.
That use is not forbidden usury,
Which happies those that pay the willing loan;
That's for thyself to breed another thee,
Or ten times happier, be it ten for one;
Ten times thyself were happier than thou art,
If ten of thine ten times refigured thee:
Then what could death do, if thou shouldst depart,
Leaving thee living in posterity?
    Be not self-will'd, for thou art much too fair
    To be death's conquest and make worms thine heir.

7

Lo, in the orient when the gracious light
Lifts up his burning head, each under eye
Doth homage to his new-appearing sight,
Serving with looks his sacred majesty;
And having climb'd the steep-up heavenly hill,
Resembling strong youth in his middle age,
Yet mortal looks adore his beauty still,
Attending on his golden pilgrimage;
But when from highmost pitch, with weary car,
Like feeble age, he reeleth from the day,
The eyes, 'fore duteous, now converted are
From his low tract and look another way:
  So thou, thyself outgoing in thy noon,
  Unlookt on diest, unless thou get a son.

8

Music to hear, why hear'st thou music sadly?
Sweets with sweets war not, joy delights in joy.
Why lovest thou that which thou receivest not gladly,
Or else receivest with pleasure thine annoy?
If the true concord of well-tuned sounds,
By unions married, do offend thine ear,
They do but sweetly chide thee, who confounds
In singleness the parts that thou shouldst bear.
Mark how one string, sweet husband to another,
Strikes each in each by mutual ordering;
Resembling sire and child and happy mother,
Who, all in one, one pleasing note do sing:
  Whose speechless song, being many, seeming one,
  Sings this to thee, 'Thou single wilt prove none.'

9

Is it for fear to wet a widow's eye
That thou consumest thyself in single life?
Ah! if thou issueless shalt hap to die,
The world will wail thee, like a makeless wife;
The world will be thy widow, and still weep
That thou no form of thee hast left behind,
When every private widow well may keep
By children's eyes her husband's shape in mind.
Look, what an unthrift in the world doth spend
Shifts but his place, for still the world enjoys it;
But beauty's waste hath in the world an end,
And kept unused, the user so destroys it.
  No love toward others in that bosom sits
  That on himself such murd'rous shame commits.

10

For shame deny that thou bear'st love to any,
Who for thyself art so unprovident.
Grant, if thou wilt, thou art beloved of many,
But that thou none lovest is most evident;
For thou art possest with murd'rous hate,
That 'gainst thyself thou stick'st not to conspire,
Seeking that beauteous roof to ruinate,
Which to repair should be thy chief desire.
O, change thy thought, that I may change my mind!
Shall hate be fairer lodged than gentle love?
Be, as thy presence is, gracious and kind,
Or to thyself, at least, kind-hearted prove:
    Make thee another self, for love of me,
    That beauty still may live in thine or thee.

11

As fast as thou shalt wane, so fast thou grow'st
In one of thine, from that which thou departest;
And that fresh blood which youngly thou bestow'st
Thou mayst call thine when thou from youth convertest.
Herein lives wisdom, beauty, and increase;
Without this, folly, age, and cold decay:
If all were minded so, the times should cease,
And threescore year would make the world away.
Let those whom Nature hath not made for store,
Harsh, featureless, and rude, barrenly perish:
Look, whom she best endow'd she gave the more;
Which bounteous gift thou shouldst in bounty cherish:
    She carved thee for her seal, and meant thereby
    Thou shouldst print more, not let that copy die.

12

When I do count the clock that tells the time,
And see the brave day sunk in hideous night;
When I behold the violet past prime,
And sable curls all silver'd o'er with white;
When lofty trees I see barren of leaves,
Which erst from heat did canopy the herd,
And summer's green, all girded up in sheaves,
Borne on the bier with white and bristly beard;
Then of thy beauty do I question make,
That thou among the wastes of time must go,
Since sweets and beauties do themselves forsake,
And die as fast as they see others grow;
    And nothing 'gainst Time's scythe can make defence
    Save breed, to brave him when he takes thee hence.

13

O that you were yourself! but, love, you are
No longer yours than you yourself here live:
Against this coming end you should prepare,
And your sweet semblance to some other give.
So should that beauty which you hold in lease
Find no determination; then you were
Yourself again, after yourself's decease,
When your sweet issue your sweet form should bear.
Who lets so fair a house fall to decay,
Which husbandry in honour might uphold
Against the stormy gusts of winter's day
And barren rage of death's eternal cold?
    O, none but unthrifts: dear my love, you know
    You had a father; let your son say so.

14

Not from the stars do I my judgement pluck;
And yet methinks I have astronomy,
But not to tell of good or evil luck,
Of plagues, of dearths, or seasons' quality;
Nor can I fortune to brief minutes tell,
Pointing to each his thunder, rain and wind,
Or say with princes if it shall go well,
By oft predict that I in heaven find:
But from thine eyes my knowledge I derive,
And, constant stars, in them I read such art,
As truth and beauty shall together thrive,
If from thyself to store thou wouldst convert;
    Or else of thee this I prognosticate:
    They end is truth's and beauty's doom and date.

15

When I consider every thing that grows
Holds in perfection but a little moment,
That this huge stage presenteth naught but shows
Whereon the stars in secret influence comment;
When I perceive that men as plants increase,
Cheered and checkt even by the self-same sky,
Vaunt in their youthful sap, at height decrease,
And wear their brave state out of memory;
Then the conceit of this inconstant stay
Sets you most rich in youth before my sight,
Where wasteful Time debateth with Decay,
To change your day of youth to sullied night;
    And, all in war with Time, for love of you,
    As he takes from you, I engraft you new.

16

But wherefore do not you a mightier way
Make war upon this bloody tyrant, Time?
And fortify yourself in your decay
With means more blessed than my barren rime?
Now stand you on the top of happy hours;
And many maiden gardens, yet unset,
With virtuous wish would bear your living flowers,
Much liker than your painted counterfeit:
So should the lines of life that life repair,
Which this, Time's pencil, or my pupil pen,
Neither in inward worth nor outward fair,
Can make you live yourself in eyes of men.
    To give away yourself keeps yourself still;
    And you must live, drawn by your own sweet skill.

17

Who will believe my verse in time to come,
If it were fill'd with your most high deserts?
Though yet, heaven knows, it is but as a tomb
Which hides your life, and shows not half your parts.
If I could write the beauty of your eyes,
And in fresh numbers number all your graces,
The age to come would say, 'This poet lies,
Such heavenly touches ne'er toucht earthly faces.'
So should my papers, yellow'd with their age,
Be scorn'd, like old men of less truth than tongue;
And your true rights be term'd a poet's rage,
And stretched metre of an antique song:
    But were some child of yours alive that time,
    You should live twice, in it and in my rime.

18

Shall I compare thee to a summer's day?
Thou art more lovely and more temperate:
Rough winds do shake the darling buds of May,
And summer's lease hath all too short a date:
Sometime too hot the eye of heaven shines,
And often is his gold complexion dimm'd;
And every fair from fair sometime declines,
By chance, or nature's changing course, untrimm'd;
But thy eternal summer shall not fade,
Nor lose possession of that fair thou ow'st;
Nor shall Death brag thou wander'st in his shade,
When in eternal lines to time thou grow'st:
    So long as men can breathe, or eyes can see,
    So long lives this, and this gives life to thee.

19

Devouring Time, blunt thou the lion's paws,
And make the earth devour her own sweet brood;
Pluck the keen teeth from the fierce tiger's jaws,
And burn the long-lived phoenix in her blood;
Make glad and sorry seasons as thou fleets,
And do whate'er thou wilt, swift-footed Time,
To the wide world and all her fading sweets;
But I forbid thee one most heinous crime:
O, carve not with thy hours my love's fair brow,
Nor draw no lines there with thine antique pen;
Him in thy course untainted do allow
For beauty's pattern to succeeding men.
    Yet, do thy worst, old Time: despite thy wrong,
    My love shall in my verse ever live young.

20

A woman's face, with Nature's own hand painted,
Hast thou, the master-mistress of my passion;
A woman's gentle heart, but not acquainted
With shifting change, as is false women's fashion;
An eye more bright than theirs, less false in rolling,
Gilding the object whereupon it gazeth;
A man in hew all *Hews* in his controlling,
Which steals men's eyes, and women's souls amazeth.
And for a woman wert thou first created;
Till Nature, as she wrought thee, fell a-doting,
And by addition me of thee defeated,
By adding one thing to my purpose nothing.
    But since she prickt thee out for women's pleasure,
    Mine be thy love, and thy love's use their treasure.

21

So is it not with me as with that Muse.
Stirr'd by a painted beauty to his verse,
Who heaven itself for ornament doth use,
And every fair with his fair doth rehearse;
Making a couplement of proud compare,
With sun and moon, with earth and sea's rich gems,
With April's first-born flowers, and all things rare
That heaven's air in this huge rondure hems.
O, let me, true in love, but truly write,
And then believe me, my love is as fair
As any mother's child, though not so bright
As those gold candles fixt in heaven's air:
    Let them say more that like of hearsay well;
    I will not praise that purpose not to sell.

22

My glass shall not persuade me I am old,
So long as youth and thou are of one date;
But when in thee time's furrows I behold,
Then look I death my days should expiate.
For all that beauty that doth cover thee
Is but the seemly raiment of my heart,
Which in my breast doth live, as thine in me:
How can I, then, be elder than thou art?
O, therefore, love, be of thyself so wary
As I, not for myself, but for thee will;
Bearing thy heart, which I will keep so chary
As tender nurse her babe from faring ill.
    Presume not on thy heart when mine is slain;.
    Thou gavest me thine, not to give back again.

23

As an unperfect actor on the stage,
Who, with his fear is put besides his part,
Or some fierce thing replete with too much rage,
Whose strength's abundance weakens his own heart;
So I, for fear of trust, forget to say
The perfect ceremony of love's rite,
And in mine own love's strength seem to decay,
O'ercharged with burthen of mine own love's might.
O, let my books be, then, the eloquence
And dumb presagers of my speaking breast;
Who plead for love, and look for recompense,
More than that tongue that more hath more exprest.
    O, learn to read what silent love hath writ:
    To hear with eyes belongs to love's fine wit.

24

Mine eye hath play'd the painter, and hath stell'd
Thy beauty's form in table of my heart;
My body is the frame wherein 'tis held,
And perspective it is best painter's art.
For through the painter must you see his skill,
To find where your true image pictured lies;
Which in my bosom's shop is hanging still,
That hath his windows glazed with thine eyes.
Now see what good turns eyes for eyes have done:
Mine eyes have drawn thy shape, and thine for me
Are windows to my breast, where-through the sun
Delights to peep, to gaze therein on thee;
    Yet eyes this cunning want to grace their art,
    They draw but what they see, know not the heart.

25

Let those who are in favour with their stars
Of public honour and proud titles boast,
Whilst I, whom fortune of such triumph bars,
Unlookt for joy in that I honour most.
Great princes' favourites their fair leaves spread
But as the marigold at the sun's eye;
And in themselves their pride lies buried,
For at a frown they in their glory die.
The painful warrior famoused for fight,
After a thousand victories once foil'd,
Is from the book of honour razed quite,
And all the rest forgot for which he toil'd:
    Then happy I, that love and am beloved
    Where I may not remove nor be removed.

26

Lord of my love, to whom in vassalage
Thy merit hath my duty strongly knit,
To thee I send this written ambassage,
To witness duty, not to show my wit:
Duty so great, which wit so poor as mine
May make seem bare, in wanting words to show it,
But that I hope some good conceit of thine
In thy soul's thought, all naked, will bestow it;
Till whatsoever star that guides my moving,
Points on me graciously with fair aspect,
And puts apparel on my totter'd loving,
To show me worthy of thy sweet respect:
    Then may I dare to boast how I do love thee;
    Till then not show my head where thou mayst prove me.

27

Weary with toil, I haste me to my bed,
The dear repose for limbs with travel tired;
But then begins a journey in my head,
To work my mind, when body's work's expired:
For then my thoughts, from far where I abide,
Intend a zealous pilgrimage to thee,
And keep my drooping eyelids open wide,
Looking on darkness which the blind do see:
Save that my soul's imaginary sight
Presents thy shadow to my sightless view,
Which, like a jewel hung in ghostly night,
Makes black night beauteous, and her old face new.
    Lo, thus, by day my limbs, by night my mind,
    For thee and for myself no quiet find.

28

How can I, then, return in happy plight,
That am debarr'd the benefit of rest?
When day's oppression is not eased by night,
But day by night, and night by day, opprest?
And each, though enemies to either's reign,
Do in consent shake hands to torture me;
The one by toil, the other to complain
How far I toil, still farther off from thee.
I tell the day, to please him thou art bright,
And dost him grace when clouds do blot the heaven:
So flatter I the swart-complexion'd night,
When sparkling stars twire not thou gild'st the even.
 But day doth daily draw my sorrows longer,
 And night doth nightly make grief's strength seem stronger.

29

When, in disgrace with fortune and men's eyes,
I all alone beweep my outcast state,
And trouble deaf heaven with my bootless cries,
And look upon myself, and curse my fate,
Wishing me like to one more rich in hope,
Featured like him, like him with friends possest,
Desiring this man's art, and that man's scope,
With what I most enjoy contented least;
Yet in these thoughts myself almost despising,
Haply I think on thee, – and then my state,
Like to the lark at break of day arising
From sullen earth, sings hymns at heaven's gate;
 For thy sweet love remember'd such wealth brings,
 That then I scorn to change my state with kings.

30

When to the sessions of sweet silent thought
I summon up remembrance of things past,
I sigh the lack of many a thing I sought,
And with old woes new wail my dear time's waste:
Then can I drown an eye, unused to flow,
For precious friends hid in death's dateless night,
And weep afresh love's long-since-cancell'd woe,
And moan the expense of many a vanisht sight:
Then can I grieve at grievances foregone,
And heavily from woe to woe tell o'er
The sad account of fore-bemoaned moan,
Which I new pay as if not paid before.
 But if the while I think on thee, dear friend,
 All losses are restored, and sorrows end.

31

Thy bosom is endeared with all hearts,
Which I by lacking have supposed dead;
And there reigns love, and all love's loving parts,
And all those friends which I thought buried.
How many a holy and obsequious tear
Hath dear religious love stoln from my eye,
As interest of the dead, which now appear
But things removed, that hidden in thee lie!
Thou art the grave where buried love doth live,
Hung with the trophies of my lovers gone,
Who all their parts of me to thee did give;
That due of many now is thine alone:
    Their images I loved I view in thee,
    And thou, all they, hast all the all of me.

32

If thou survive my well-contented day,
When that churl Death my bones with dust shall cover,
And shalt by fortune once more re-survey
These poor rude lines of thy deceased lover:
Compare them with the bettering of the time,
And though they be outstript by every pen,
Reserve them for my love, not for their rime,
Exceeded by the height of happier men.
O, then vouchsafe me but this loving thought:
'Had my friend's Muse grown with this growing age,
A dearer birth than this his love had brought,
To march in ranks of better equipage:
    But since he died, and poets better prove,
    Theirs for their style I'll read, his for his love.'

33

Full many a glorious morning have I seen
Flatter the mountain-tops with sovereign eye,
Kissing with golden face the meadows green,
Gilding pale streams with heavenly alchemy;
Anon permit the basest clouds to ride
With ugly rack on his celestial face,
And from the forlorn world his visage hide,
Stealing unseen to west with this disgrace:
Even so my sun one early morn did shine
With all-triumphant splendour on my brow;
But, out, alack! he was but one hour mine,
The region cloud hath maskt him from me now.
    Yet him for this my love no whit disdaineth;
    Suns of the world may stain when heaven's sun staineth.

34

Why didst thou promise such a beauteous day,
And make me travel forth without my cloak,
To let base clouds o'ertake me in my way,
Hiding thy bravery in their rotten smoke?
'Tis not enough that through the cloud thou break,
To dry the rain on my storm-beaten face,
For no man well of such a salve can speak
That heals the wound, and cures not the disgrace:
Nor can thy shame give physic to my grief;
Though thou repent, yet I have still the loss:
The offender's sorrow lends but weak relief
To him that bears the strong offence's cross.
    Ah, but those tears are pearl which thy love sheeds,
    And they are rich, and ransom all ill deeds.

35

No more be grieved at that which thou hast done:
Roses have thorns, and silver fountains mud;
Clouds and eclipses stain both moon and sun,
And loathsome canker lives in sweetest bud.
All men make faults, and even I in this,
Authorizing thy trespass with compare,
Myself corrupting, salving thy amiss,
Excusing 'their sins more than thy sins are';
For to thy sensual fault I bring in sense, –
Thy adverse party is thy advocate, –
And 'gainst myself a lawful plea commence:
Such civil war is in my love and hate,
    That I an accessary needs must be
    To that sweet thief which sourly robs from me.

36

Let me confess that we two must be twain,
Although our undivided loves are one:
So shall those blots that do with me remain,
Without thy help, by me be borne alone.
In our two loves there is but one respect,
Though in our lives a separable spite,
Which though it alter not love's sole effect,
Yet doth it steal sweet hours from love's delight.
I may not evermore acknowledge thee,
Lest my bewailed guilt should do thee shame;
Nor thou with public kindness honour me,
Unless thou take that honour from thy name:
    But do not so; I love thee in such sort,
    As, thou being mine, mine is thy good report.

37

As a decrepit father takes delight
To see his active child do deeds of youth,
So I, made lame by Fortune's dearest spite,
Take all my comfort of thy worth and truth;
For whether beauty, birth, or wealth, or wit,
Or any of these all, or all, or more,
Entitled in their parts do crowned sit,
I make my love engrafted to this store:
So then I am not lame, poor, nor despised,
Whilst that this shadow doth such substance give
That I in thy abundance am sufficed,
And by a part of all thy glory live.
    Look, what is best, that best I wish in thee:
    This wish I have; then ten times happy me!

38

How can my Muse want subject to invent,
While thou dost breathe, that pour'st into my verse
Thine own sweet argument, too excellent
For every vulgar paper to rehearse?
O, give thyself the thanks, if aught in me
Worthy perusal stand against thy sight;
For who's so dumb that cannot write to thee,
When thou thyself dost give invention light?
Be thou the tenth Muse, ten times more in worth
Than those old nine which rimers invocate;
And he that calls on thee, let him bring forth
Eternal numbers to outlive long date.
    If my slight Muse do please these curious days,
    The pain be mine, but thine shall be the praise.

39

O, how thy worth with manners may I sing,
When thou art all the better part of me?
What can mine own praise to mine own self bring?
And what is't but mine own when I praise thee?
Even for this let us divided live,
And our dear love lose name of single one,
That by this separation I may give
That due to thee which thou deservest alone.
O absence, what a torment wouldst thou prove,
Were it not thy sour leisure gave sweet leave
To entertain the time with thoughts of love,
Which time and thoughts so sweetly doth deceive,
    And that thou teachest how to make one twain,
    By praising him here who doth hence remain!

40

Take all my loves, my love, yea, take them all;
What hast thou then more than thou hadst before?
No love, my love, that thou mayst true love call;
All mine was thine before thou hadst this more.
Then, if for my love thou my love receivest,
I cannot blame thee for my love thou usest;
But yet be blamed, if thou this self deceivest
By wilful taste of what thyself refusest.
I do forgive thy robbery, gentle thief,
Although thou steal thee all my poverty;
And yet, love knows, it is a greater grief
To bear love's wrong than hate's known injury.
    Lascivious grace, in whom all ill well shows,
    Kill me with spites; yet we must not be foes.

41

Those pretty wrongs that liberty commits,
When I am sometime absent from thy heart,
Thy beauty and thy years full well befits,
For still temptation follows where thou art.
Gentle thou art, and therefore to be won,
Beauteous thou art, therefore to be assailed;
And when a woman woos, what woman's son
Will sourly leave her till she have prevailed?
Ay me! but yet thou mightst my seat forbear,
And chide thy beauty and thy straying youth,
Who lead thee in their riot even there
Where thou art forced to break a twofold truth, –
    Hers, by thy beauty tempting her to thee,
    Thine, by thy beauty being false to me.

42

That thou hast her, it is not all my grief,
And yet it may be said I loved her dearly;
That she hath thee, is of my wailing chief,
A loss in love that touches me more nearly.
Loving offenders, thus I will excuse ye: –
Thou dost love her, because thou know'st I love her;
And for my sake even so doth she abuse me,
Suff'ring my friend for my sake to approve her.
If I lose thee, my loss is my love's gain,
And losing her, my friend hath found that loss;
Both find each other, and I lose both twain,
And both for my sake lay on me this cross:
    But here's the joy; my friend and I are one;
    Sweet flattery! then she loves but me alone.

43

When most I wink, then do mine eyes best see,
For all the day they view things unrespected;
But when I sleep, in dreams they look on thee,
And, darkly bright, are bright in dark directed.
Then thou, whose shadow shadows doth make bright
How would thy shadow's form form happy show
To the clear day with thy much clearer light,
When to unseeing eyes thy shade shines so!
How would, I say, mine eyes be blessed made
By looking on thee in the living day,
When in dead night thy fair imperfect shade
Through heavy sleep on sightless eyes doth stay
    All days are nights to see till I see thee,
    And nights bright days when dreams do show thee me.

44

If the dull substance of my flesh were thought,
Injurious distance should not stop my way;
For then, despite of space, I would be brought,
From limits far remote, where thou dost stay.
No matter then although my foot did stand
Upon the farthest earth removed from thee;
For nimble thought can jump both sea and land
As soon as think the place where he would be.
But, ah, thought kills me, that I am not thought,
To leap large lengths of miles when thou art gone,
But that, so much of earth and water wrought,
I must attend time's leisure with my moan;
    Receiving naught by elements so slow
    But heavy tears, badges of either's woe.

45

The other two, slight air and purging fire,
Are both with thee, wherever I abide;
The first my thought, the other my desire,
These present-absent with swift motion slide.
For when these quicker elements are gone
In tender embassy of love to thee,
My life, being made of four, with two alone
Sinks down to death, opprest with melancholy;
Until life's composition be recured
By those swift messengers return'd from thee,
Who even but now come back again, assured
Of thy fair health, recounting it to me:
    This told, I joy; but then no longer glad,
    I send them back again, and straight grow sad.

46

Mine eye and heart are at a mortal war,
How to divide the conquest of thy sight;
Mine eye my heart thy picture's sight would bar,
My heart mine eye the freedom of that right.
My heart doth plead that thou in him dost lie –
A closet never pierced with crystal eyes –
But the defendant doth that plea deny,
And says in him thy fair appearance lies.
To cide this title is impanneled
A quest of thoughts, all tenants to the heart;
And by their verdict is determined
The clear eye's moiety and the dear heart's part:
    As thus; mine eye's due is thy outward part,
    And my heart's right thy inward love of heart.

47

Betwixt mine eye and heart a league is took,
And each doth good turns now unto the other:
When that mine eye is famisht for a look,
Or heart in love with sighs himself doth smother,
With my love's picture then my eye doth feast,
And to the painted banquet bids my heart;
Another time mine eye is my heart's guest,
And in his thoughts of love doth share a part:
So, either by thy picture or my love,
Thyself away art present still with me;
For thou not farther than my thoughts canst move,
And I am still with them, and they with thee;
    Or, if they sleep, thy picture in my sight
    Awakes my heart to heart's and eye's delight.

48

How careful was I, when I took my way,
Each trifle under truest bars to thrust,
That to my use it might unused stay
From hands of falsehood, in sure wards of trust!
But thou, to whom my jewels trifles are,
Most worthy comfort, now my greatest grief,
Thou, best of dearest, and mine only care,
Art left the prey of every vulgar thief.
Thee have I not lockt up in any chest,
Save where thou art not, though I feel thou art,
Within the gentle closure of my breast,
From whence at pleasure thou mayst come and part;
    And even thence thou wilt be stoln, I fear,
    For truth proves thievish for a prize so dear.

49

Against that time, if ever that time come,
When I shall see thee frown on my defects,
Whenas thy love hath cast his utmost sum,
Call'd to that audit by advised respects;
Against that time when thou shalt strangely pass,
And scarcely greet me with that sun, thine eye,
When love, converted from the thing it was,
Shall reasons find of settled gravity;
Against that time do I ensconce me here
Within the knowledge of mine own desert,
And this my hand against myself uprear,
To guard the lawful reasons on thy part:
    To leave poor me thou hast the strength of laws,
    Since why to love I can allege no cause.

50

How heavy do I journey on the way,
When what I seek – my weary travel's end –
Doth teach that ease and that repose to say,
'Thus far the miles are measured from thy friend!'
The beast that bears me, tired with my woe,
Plods dully on, to bear that weight in me,
As if by some instinct the wretch did know
His rider loved not speed, being made from thee:
The bloody spur cannot provoke him on
That sometimes anger thrusts into his hide;
Which heavily he answers with a groan,
More sharp to me than spurring to his side;
    For that same groan doth put this in my mind;
    My grief lies onward, and my joy behind.

51

Thus can my love excuse the slow offence
Of my dull bearer when from thee I speed:
From where thou art why should I haste me thence?
Till I return, of posting is no need.
O, what excuse will my poor beast then find,
When swift extremity can seem but slow?
Then should I spur, though mounted on the wind,
In winged speed no motion shall I know:
Then can no horse with my desire keep pace;
Therefore desire, of perfect'st love being made,
Shall neigh, no dull flesh in his fiery race;
But love, for love, thus shall excuse my jade, –
    Since from thee going he went wilful-slow,
    Towards thee I'll run, and give him leave to go.

52

So am I as the rich, whose blessed key
Can bring him to his sweet up-locked treasure,
The which he will not every hour survey,
For blunting the fine point of seldom pleasure.
Therefore are feasts so solemn and so rare,
Since, seldom coming, in the long year set,
Like stones of worth they thinly placed are,
Or captain jewels in the carcanet.
So is the time that keeps you, as my chest,
Or as the wardrobe which the robe doth hide,
To make some special instant special blest,
By new unfolding his imprison'd pride.
    Blessed are you, whose worthiness gives scope,
    Being had, to triumph, being lackt, to hope.

53

What is your substance, whereof are you made,
That millions of strange shadows on you tend?
Since every one hath, every one, one shade,
And you, but one, can every shadow lend.
Describe Adonis, and the counterfeit
Is poorly imitated after you;
On Helen's cheek all art of beauty set,
And you in Grecian tires are painted new:
Speak of the spring, and foison of the year;
The one doth shadow of your beauty show,
The other as your bounty doth appear;
And you in every blessed shape we know.
    In all external grace you have some part,
    But you like none, none you, for constant heart.

54

O, how much more doth beauty beauteous seem
By that sweet ornament which truth doth give!
The rose looks fair, but fairer we it deem
For that sweet odour which doth in it live.
The canker-blooms have full as deep a dye
As the perfumed tincture of the roses,
Hang on such thorns, and play as wantonly
When summer's breath their masked buds discloses:
But, for their virtue only is their show,
They live unwoo'd, and unrespected fade;
Die to themselves. Sweet roses do not so;
Of their sweet deaths are sweetest odours made:
    And so of you, beauteous and lovely youth,
    When that shall vade, my verse distils your truth.

55

Not marble, nor the gilded monuments
Of princes, shall outlive this powerful rime;
But you shall shine more bright in these contents
Than unswept stone, besmear'd with sluttish time.
When wasteful war shall statues overturn,
And broils root out the work of masonry,
Nor Mars his sword nor war's quick fire shall burn
The living record of your memory.
'Gainst death and all-oblivious enmity
Shall you pace forth; your praise shall still find room
Even in the eyes of all posterity
That wears this world out to the ending doom.
    So, till the judgement that yourself arise,
    You live in this, and dwell in lovers' eyes.

56

Sweet love, renew thy force; be it not said
Thy edge should blunter be than appetite,
Which but to-day by feeding is allay'd,
To-morrow sharpen'd in his former might:
So, love, be thou; although to-day thou fill
Thy hungry eyes even till they wink with fullness,
To-morrow see again, and do not kill
The spirit of love with a perpetual dullness.
Let this sad int'rim like the ocean be
Which parts the shore, where two contracted new
Come daily to the banks, that, when they see
Return of love, more blest may be the view;
    Or call it winter, which, being full of care,
    Makes summer's welcome thrice more wisht, more rare.

57

Being your slave, what should I do but tend
Upon the hours and times of your desire?
I have no precious time at all to spend,
Nor services to do, till you require.
Nor dare I chide the world-without-end hour
Whilst I, my sovereign, watch the clock for you,
Nor think the bitterness of absence sour
When you have bid your servant once adieu;
Nor dare I question with my jealous thought
Where you may be, or your affairs suppose,
But, like a sad slave, stay and think of nought
Save, where you are how happy you make those.
    So true a fool is love, that in your Will,
    Though you do any thing, he thinks no ill.

58

That god forbid that made-me first your slave,
I should in thought control your times of pleasure,
Or at your hand the account of hours to crave,
Being your vassal, bound to stay your leisure!
O, let me suffer, being at your beck,
The imprison'd absence of your liberty;
And patience, tame to sufferance, bide each check,
Without accusing you of injury.
Be where you list, your charter is so strong,
That you yourself may privilege your time
To what you will; to you it doth belong
Yourself to pardon of self-doing crime.
　　I am to wait, though waiting so be hell;
　　Not blame your pleasure, be it ill or well.

59

If there be nothing new, but that which is
Hath been before, how are our brains beguiled,
Which, labouring for invention, bear amiss
The second burden of a former child!
O, That record could with a backward look,
Even of five hundred courses of the sun,
Show me your image in some antique book,
Since mind at first in character was done!
That I might see what the old world could say
To this composed wonder of your frame;
Whether we are mended, or whe'r better they,
Or whether revolution be the same.
　　O, sure I am, the wits of former days
　　To subjects worse have given admiring praise.

60

Like as the waves make towards the pebbled shore,
So do our minutes hasten to their end;
Each changing place with that which goes before,
In sequent toil all forwards do contend.
Nativity, once in the main of light,
Crawls to maturity, wherewith being crown'd,
Crooked eclipses 'gainst his glory fight,
And Time that gave doth now his gift confound.
Time doth transfix the flourish set on youth,
And delves the parallels in beauty's brow;
Feeds on the rarities of nature's truth,
And nothing stands but for his scythe to mow:
　　And yet, to times in hope my verse shall stand,
　　Praising thy worth, despite his cruel hand.

61

Is it thy will thy image should keep open
My heavy eyelids to the weary night?
Dost thou desire my slumbers should be broken,
While shadows like to thee do mock my sight?
Is it thy spirit that thou send'st from thee
So far from home into my deeds to pry,
To find out shames and idle hours in me,
The scope and tenour of thy jealousy?
O, no! thy love, though much, is not so great:
It is my love that keeps mine eye awake;
Mine own true love that doth my rest defeat,
To play the watchman ever for thy sake:
    For thee watch I whilst thou dost wake elsewhere,
    From me far off, with others all too near.

62

Sin of self-love possesseth all mine eye,
And all my soul, and all my every part;
And for this sin there is no remedy,
It is so grounded inward in my heart.
Methinks no face so gracious is as mine,
No shape so true, no truth of such account;
And for myself mine own worth do define,
As I all other in all worths surmount.
But when my glass shows me myself indeed,
Beated and chopt with tann'd antiquity,
Mine own self-love quite contrary I read;
Self so self-loving were iniquity.
    'Tis thee, myself, that for myself I praise,
    Painting my age with beauty of thy days.

63

Against my love shall be, as I am now,
With Time's injurious hand crusht and o'erworn;
When hours have drain'd his blood, and fill'd his brow
With lines and wrinkles; when his youthful morn
Hath travell'd on to age's steepy night;
And all those beauties whereof now he's king
Are vanishing or vanisht out of sight,
Stealing away the treasure of his spring;
For such a time do I now fortify
Against confounding age's cruel knife,
That he shall never cut from memory
My sweet love's beauty, though my lover's life:
    His beauty shall in these black lines be seen,
    And they shall live, and he in them still green.

64

When I have seen by Time's fell hand defaced
The rich proud cost of outworn buried age;
When sometime lofty towers I see down-razed,
And brass eternal slave to mortal rage;
When I have seen the hungry ocean gain
Advantage on the kingdom of the shore,
And the firm soil win of the watery main,
Increasing store with loss, and loss with store;
When I have seen such interchange of state,
Or state itself confounded to decay;
Ruin hath taught me thus to ruminate, –
That Time will come and take my love away.
   This thought is as a death, which cannot choose
   But weep to have that which it fears to lose.

65

Since brass, nor stone, nor earth, nor boundless sea,
But sad mortality o'ersways their power,
How with this rage shall beauty hold a plea,
Whose action is no stronger than a flower?
O, how shall summer's honey breath hold out
Against the wrackful siege of battering days,
When rocks impregnable are not so stout,
Nor gates of steel so strong, but Time decays?
O fearful meditation! where, alack,
Shall Time's best jewel from Time's chest lie hid?
Or what strong hand can hold his swift foot back?
Or who his spoil of beauty can forbid?
   O, none, unless this miracle have might,
   That in black ink my love may still shine bright.

66

Tired with all these, for restful death I cry, –
As, to behold Desert a beggar born,
And needy Nothing trimm'd in jollity,
And purest Faith unhappily forsworn,
And gilded Honour shamefully misplaced,
And maiden Virtue rudely strumpeted,
And right Perfection wrongfully disgraced,
And Strength by limping Sway disabled,
And Art made tongue-tied by Authority,
And Folly, doctor-like, controlling Skill,
And simple Truth miscall'd Simplicity,
And captive Good attending captain Ill:
   Tired with all these, from these would I be gone,
   Save that, to die, I leave my love alone.

67

Ah, wherefore with infection should he live,
And with his presence grace impiety,
That sin by him advantage should achieve,
And lace itself with his society?
Why should false painting imitate his cheek,
And steal dead seeing of his living hue?
Why should poor beauty indirectly seek
Roses of shadow, since his rose is true?
Why should he live, now Nature bankrout is,
Beggar'd of blood to blush through lively veins?
For she hath no exchequer now but his,
And, proud of many, lives upon his gains.
    O, him she stores, to show what wealth she had
    In days long since, before these last so bad.

68

Thus is his cheek the map of days outworn,
When beauty lived and died as flowers do now,
Before these bastard signs of fair were born,
Or durst inhabit on a living brow;
Before the golden tresses of the dead,
The right of sepulchres, were shorn away,
To live a second life on second head;
Ere beauty's dead fleece made another gay:
In him those holy antique hours are seen,
Without all ornament, itself, and true,
Making no summer of another's green,
Robbing no old to dress his beauty new;
    And him as for a map doth Nature store,
    To show false Art what beauty was of yore.

69

Those parts of thee that the world's eye doth view
Want nothing that the thought of hearts can mend;
All tongues, the voice of souls, give thee that due,
Uttering bare truth, even so as foes commend.
Thy outward thus with outward praise is crown'd;
But those same tongues, that give thee so thine own,
In other accents do this praise confound
By seeing farther than the eye hath shown.
They look into the beauty of thy mind,
And that, in guess, they measure by thy deeds;
Then, churls, their thoughts, although their eyes were kind
To thy fair flower add the rank smell of weeds:
    But why thy odour matcheth not thy show,
    The soil is this, that thou dost common grow.

70

That thou art blamed shall not be thy defect,
For slander's mark was ever yet the fair;
The ornament of beauty is suspect,
A crow that flies in heaven's sweetest air.
So thou be good, slander doth but approve
Thy worth the greater, being woo'd of time;
For canker vice the sweetest buds doth love,
And thou present'st a pure unstained prime.
Thou hast past by the ambush of young days,
Either not assail'd, or victor being charged;
Yet this thy praise cannot be so thy praise,
To tie up envy evermore enlarged:
    If some suspect of ill maskt not thy show,
    Then thou alone kingdoms of hearts shouldst owe.

71

No longer mourn for me when I am dead
Than you shall hear the surly sullen bell
Give warning to the world that I am fled
From this vile world, with vilest worms to dwell:
Nay, if you read this line, remember not
The hand that writ it; for I love you so,
That I in your sweet thoughts would be forgot,
If thinking on me then should make you woe.
O, if I say, you look upon this verse
When I perhaps compounded am with clay,
Do not so much as my poor name rehearse;
But let your love even with my life decay;
    Lest the wise world should look into your moan,
    And mock you with me after I am gone.

72

O, lest the world should task you to recite
What merit lived in me, that you should love,
After my death, dear love, forget me quite,
For you in me can nothing worthy prove;
Unless you would devise some virtuous lie,
To do more for me than mine own desert,
And hang more praise upon deceased I
Than niggard truth would willingly impart:
O, lest your true love may seem false in this,
That you for love speak well of me untrue,
My name be buried where my body is,
And live no more to shame nor me nor you.
    For I am shamed by that which I bring forth,
    And so should you, to love things nothing worth.

73

That time of year thou mayst in me behold
When yellow leaves, or none, or few, do hang
Upon those boughs which shake against the cold,
Bare ruin'd choirs, where late the sweet birds sang.
In me thou see'st the twilight of such day
As after sunset fadeth in the west;
Which by and by black night doth take away,
Death's second self, that seals up all in rest.
In me thou see'st the glowing of such fire,
That on the ashes of his youth doth lie,
As the death-bed whereon it must expire,
Consumed with that which it was nourisht by.
    This thou perceivest, which makes thy love more strong,
    To love that well which thou must leave ere long.

74

But be contented: when that fell arrest
Without all bail shall carry me away,
My life hath in this line some interest,
Which for memorial still with thee shall stay.
When thou reviewest this, thou dost review
The very part was consecrate to thee:
The earth can have but earth, which is his due;
My spirit is thine, the better part of me:
So, then, thou hast but lost the dregs of life,
The prey of worms, my body being dead;
The coward conquest of a wretch's knife,
Too base of thee to be remembered.
    The worth of that is that which it contains,
    And that is this, and this with thee remains.

75

So are you to my thoughts as food to life,
Or as sweet-season'd showers are to the ground;
And for the peace of you I hold such strife
As 'twixt a miser and his wealth is found;
Now proud as an enjoyer, and anon
Doubting the filching age will steal his treasure;
Now counting best to be with you alone,
Then better'd that the world may see my pleasure:
Sometime all full with feasting on your sight,
And by and by clean starved for a look;
Possessing or pursuing no delight,
Save what is had or must from you be took.
    Thus do I pine and surfeit day by day,
    Or gluttoning on all, or all away.

76

Why is my verse so barren of new pride,
So far from variation or quick change?
Why, with the time, do I not glance aside
To new-found methods and to compounds strange?
Why write I still all one, ever the same,
And keep invention in a noted weed,
That every word doth almost tell my name,
Showing their birth, and where they did proceed?
O, know, sweet love, I always write of you,
And you and love are still my argument;
So all my best is dressing old words new,
Spending again what is already spent:
    For as the sun is daily new and old,
    So is my love still telling what is told.

77

Thy glass will show thee how thy beauties wear,
Thy dial how thy precious minutes waste;
The vacant leaves thy mind's imprint will bear,
And of this book this learning mayst thou taste.
The wrinkles which thy glass will truly show,
Of mouthed graves will give thee memory;
Thou by thy dial's shady stealth mayst know
Time's thievish progress to eternity.
Look, what thy memory cannot contain,
Commit to these waste blanks, and thou shalt find
Those children nursed, deliver'd from thy brain,
To take a new acquaintance of thy mind.
    These offices, so oft as thou wilt look,
    Shall profit thee, and much enrich thy book.

78

So oft have I invoked thee for my Muse,
And found such fair assistance in my verse,
As every alien pen hath got my use,
And under thee their poesy disperse.
Thine eyes, that taught the dumb on high to sing,
And heavy ignorance aloft to fly,
Have added feathers to the learned's wing,
And given grace a double majesty.
Yet be most proud of that which I compile,
Whose influence is thine, and born of thee:
In others' works thou dost but mend the style,
And arts with thy sweet graces graced be;
    But thou art all my art, and dost advance
    As high as learning my rude ignorance.

79

Whilst I alone did call upon thy aid,
My verse alone had all thy gentle grace;
But now my gracious numbers are decay'd,
And my sick Muse doth give another place.
I grant, sweet love, thy lovely argument
Deserves the travail of a worthier pen;
Yet what of thee thy poet doth invent
He robs thee of, and pays it thee again.
He lends thee virtue, and he stole that word
From thy behaviour; beauty doth he give,
And found it in thy cheek; he can afford
No praise to thee but what in thee doth live.
    Then thank him not for that which he doth say,
    Since what he owes thee thou thyself dost pay.

80

O, how I faint when I of you do write,
Knowing a better spirit doth use your name,
And in the praise thereof spends all his might,
To make me tongue-tied, speaking of your fame!
But since your worth, wide as the ocean is,
The humble as the proudest sail doth bear,
My saucy bark, inferior far to his,
On your broad main doth wilfully appear.
Your shallowest help will hold me up afloat,
While he upon your soundless deep doth ride;
Or, being wrackt, I am a worthless boat,
He of tall building and of goodly pride:
    Then if he thrive, and I be cast away,
    The worst was this; my love was my decay.

81

Or I shall live your epitaph to make,
Or you survive when I in earth am rotten;
From hence your memory death cannot take,
Although in me each part will be forgotten.
Your name from hence immortal life shall have,
Though I, once gone, to all the world must die:
The earth can yield me but a common grave,
When you entombed in men's eyes shall lie.
Your monument shall be my gentle verse,
Which eyes not yet created shall o'er-read;
And tongues to be your being shall rehearse,
When all the breathers of this world are dead;
    You still shall live – such virtue hath my pen –
    Where breath most breathes, even in the mouths of men.

82

I grant thou wert not married to my Muse,
And therefore mayst without attaint o'erlook
The dedicated words which writers use
Of their fair subject, blessing every book.
Thou art as fair in knowledge as in hue,
Finding thy worth a limit past my praise;
And therefore art enforced to seek anew
Some fresher stamp of the time-bettering days.
And do so, love; yet when they have devised
What strained touches rhetoric can lend,
Thou truly fair wert truly sympathized
In true plain words by thy true-telling friend;
     And their gross painting might be better used
     Where cheeks need blood; in thee it is abused.

83

I never saw that you did painting need,
And therefore to your fair no painting set;
I found, or thought I found, you did exceed
The barren tender of a poet's debt:
And therefore have I slept in your report,
That you yourself, being extant, well might show
How far a modern quill doth come too short,
Speaking of worth, what worth in you doth grow.
This silence for my sin you did impute,
Which shall be most my glory, being dumb;
For I impair not beauty, being mute,
When others would give life, and bring a tomb.
     There lives more life in one of your fair eyes
     Than both your poets can in praise devise.

84

Who is it that? says most? which can say more
Than this rich praise, that you alone are you?
In whose confine immured is the store
Which should example where your equal grew.
Lean penury within that pen doth dwell
That to his subject lends not some small glory;
But he that writes of you, if he can tell
That you are you, so dignifies his story:
Let him but copy what in you is writ,
Not making worse what nature made so clear,
And such a counterpart shall fame his wit,
Making his style admired everywhere.
     You to your beauteous blessings add a curse,
     Being fond on praise, which makes your praises worse.

85

My tongue-tied Muse in manners holds her still,
While comments of your praise, richly compiled,
Reserve their character with golden quill,
And precious phrase by all the Muses filed.
I think good thoughts, whilst other write good words,
And, like unletter'd clerk, still cry 'Amen'
To every hymn that able spirit affords
In polish'd form of well-refined pen.
Hearing you praised, I say ' 'Tis so, 'tis true,'
And to the most of praise add something more;
But that is in my thought, whose love to you,
Though words come hindmost, holds his rank before.
　　Then others for the breath of words respect,
　　Me for my dumb thoughts, speaking in effect.

86

Was it the proud full sail of his great verse,
Bound for the prize of all-too-precious you,
That did my ripe thoughts in my brain inhearse,
Making their tomb the womb wherein they grew?
Was it his spirit, by spirits taught to write
Above a mortal pitch, that struck me dead?
No, neither he, nor his compeers by night
Giving him aid, my verse astonished.
He, nor that affable familiar ghost
Which nightly gulls him with intelligence,
As victors, of my silence cannot boast;
I was not sick of any fear from thence:
　　But when your countenance fill'd up his line,
　　Then lackt I matter; that enfeebled mine.

87

Farewell! thou art too dear for my possessing,
And like enough thou know'st thy estimate:
The charter of thy worth gives thee releasing;
My bonds in thee are all determinate.
For how do I hold thee but by thy granting?
And for that riches where is my deserving?
The cause of this fair gift in me is wanting,
And so my patent back again is swerving.
Thyself thou gavest, thy own worth then not knowing,
Or me, to whom thou gavest it, else mistaking;
So thy great gift, upon misprision growing,
Comes home again, on better judgement making
　　Thus have I had thee, as a dream doth flatter,
　　In sleep a king, but waking no such matter.

88

When thou shalt be disposed to set me light,
And place my merit in the eye of scorn,
Upon thy side against myself I'll fight,
And prove thee virtuous, though thou art forsworn.
With mine own weakness being best acquainted
Upon thy part I can set down a story
Of faults conceal'd, wherein I am attainted;
That thou, in losing me, shalt win much glory:
And I by this will be a gainer too;
For bending all my loving thoughts on thee,
The injuries that to myself I do,
Doing thee vantage, double-vantage me.
    Such is my love, to thee I so belong,
    That for thy right myself will bear all wrong.

89

Say that thou didst forsake me for some fault,
And I will comment upon that offence:
Speak of my lameness, and I straight will halt,
Against thy reasons making no defence.
Thou canst not, love, disgrace me half so ill,
To set a form upon desired change,
As I'll myself disgrace: knowing thy will,
I will acquaintance strangle, and look strange;
Be absent from thy walks; and in my tongue ;
Thy sweet beloved name no more shall dwell,
Lest I, too much profane, should do it wrong,
And haply of our old acquaintance tell.
    For thee, against myself I'll vow debate,
    For I must ne'er love him whom thou dost hate.

90

Then hate me when thou wilt; if ever, now;
Now, while the world is bent my deeds to cross,
Join with the spite of fortune, make me bow,
And do not drop in for an after-loss:
Ah, do not, when my heart hath scaped this sorrow,
Come in the rearward of a conquer'd woe;
Give not a windy night a rainy morrow,
To linger out a purposed overthrow.
If thou wilt leave me, do not leave me last,
When other petty griefs have done their spite,
But in the onset come: so shall I taste
At first the very worst of fortune's might;
    And other strains of woe, which now seem woe,
    Compared with loss of thee will not seem so.

91

Some glory in their birth, some in their skill,
Some in their wealth, some in their bodies' force;
Some in their garments, though new-fangled ill;
Some in their hawks and hounds, some in their horse;
And every humour hath his adjunct pleasure,
Wherein it finds a joy above the rest:
But these particulars are not my measure;
All these I better in one general best.
Thy love is better than high birth to me,
Richer than wealth, prouder than garments' cost,
Of more delight than hawks or horses be;
And having thee, of all men's pride I boast:
    Wretched in this alone, that thou mayst take
    All this away, and me most wretched make.

92

But do thy worst to steal thyself away,
For term of life thou art assured mine;
And life no longer than thy love will stay,
For it depends upon that love of thine.
Then need I not to fear the worst of wrongs,
When in the least of them my life hath end.
I see a better state to me belongs
Than that which on thy humour doth depend:
Thou canst not vex me with inconstant mind,
Since that my life on thy revolt doth lie.
O, what a happy title do I find,
Happy to have thy love, happy to die!
    But what's so blessed-fair that fears no blot?
    Thou mayst be false, and yet I know it not.

93

So shall I live, supposing thou art true,
Like a deceived husband; so love's face
May still seem love to me, though alter'd new;
Thy looks with me, thy heart in other place:
For there can live no hatred in thine eye,
Therefore in that I cannot know thy change.
In many's looks the false heart's history
Is writ in moods and frowns and wrinkles strange;
But heaven in thy creation did decree
That in thy face sweet love should ever dwell;
Whate'er thy thoughts or thy heart's workings be,
Thy looks should nothing thence but sweetness tell.
    How like Eve's apple doth thy beauty grow.
    If thy sweet virtue answer not thy show!

94

They that have power to hurt and will do none,
That do not do the thing they most do show,
Who, moving others, are themselves as stone,
Unmoved, cold, and to temptation slow;
They rightly do inherit heaven's graces,
And husband nature's riches from expense;
They are the lords and owners of their faces,
Others but stewards of their excellence.
The summer's flower is to the summer sweet,
Though to itself it only live and die;
But if that flower with base infection meet,
The basest weed outbraves his dignity:
    For sweetest things turn sourest by their deeds;
    Lilies that fester smell far worse than weeds.

95

How sweet and lovely dost thou make the shame
Which, like a canker in the fragrant rose,
Doth spot the beauty of thy budding name!
O, in what sweets dost thou thy sins enclose!
That tongue that tells the story of thy days,
Making lascivious comments on thy sport,
Cannot dispraise but in a kind of praise;
Naming thy name blesses an ill report.
O, what a mansion have those vices got
Which for their habitation chose out thee,
Where beauty's veil doth cover every blot,
And all things turn to fair that eyes can see!
    Take heed, dear heart, of this large privilege;
    The hardest knife ill-used doth lose his edge.

96

Some say, thy fault is youth, some wantonness;
Some say, thy grace is youth and gentle sport;
Both grace and faults are loved of more and less:
Thou makest faults graces that to thee resort.
As on the finger of a throned queen
The basest jewel will be well esteem'd,
So are those errors that in thee are seen
To truths translated, and for true things deem'd.
How many lambs might the stern wolf betray,
If like a lamb he could his looks translate!
How many gazers mightst thou lead away,
If thou wouldst use the strength of all thy state!
    But do not so; I love thee in such sort,
    As thou being mine, mine is thy good report.

97

How like a winter hath my absence been
From thee, the pleasure of the fleeting year!
What freezings have I felt, what dark days seen!
What old December's bareness every where!
And yet this time removed was summer's time;
The teeming autumn, big with rich increase,
Bearing the wanton burden of the prime,
Like widow'd wombs after their lords' decease:
Yet this abundant issue seemed to me
But hope of orphans and unfather'd fruit;
For summer and his pleasures wait on thee,
And, thou away, the very birds are mute;
    Or, if they sing, 'tis with so dull a cheer,
    That leaves look pale, dreading the winter's near.

98

From you have I been absent in the spring,
When proud-pied April, drest in all his trim,
Hath put a spirit of youth in every thing,
That heavy Saturn laught and leapt with him.
Yet nor the lays of birds, nor the sweet smell
Of different flowers in odour and in hue,
Could make me any summer's story tell,
Or from their proud lap pluck them where they grew:
Nor did I wonder at the lily's white,
Nor praise the deep vermilion in the rose;
They were but sweet, but figures of delight,
Drawn after you, – you pattern of all those.
    Yet seem'd it winter still, and, you away,
    As with your shadow I with these did play.

99

The forward violet thus did I chide:
Sweet thief, whence didst thou steal thy sweet that smells,
If not from my love's breath? The purple pride
Which on thy soft cheek for complexion dwells
In my love's veins thou hast too grossly dyed.
The lily I condemned for thy hand;
And buds of marjoram had stoln thy hair:
The roses fearfully on thorns did stand,
One blushing shame, another white despair;
A third, nor red nor white, had stoln of both,
And to his robbery had annext thy breath;
But, for his theft, in pride of all his growth
A vengeful canker eat him up to death.
    More flowers I noted, yet I none could see
    But sweet or colour it had stoln from thee.

100

Where art thou, Muse, that thou forgett'st so long
To speak of that which gives thee all thy might?
Spend'st thou thy fury on some worthless song,
Dark'ning thy power to lend base subjects light?
Return, forgetful Muse, and straight redeem
In gentle numbers time so idly spent;
Sing to the ear that doth thy lays esteem,
And gives thy pen both skill and argument.
Rise, resty Muse, my love's sweet face survey,
If Time have any wrinkle graven there;
If any, be a satire to decay,
And make Time's spoils despised everywhere.
    Give my love fame faster than Time wastes life;
    So thou prevent'st his scythe and crooked knife.

101

O truant Muse, what shall be thy amends
For thy neglect of truth in beauty dyed?
Both truth and beauty on my love depends;
So dost thou too, and therein dignified.
Make answer, Muse: wilt thou not haply say,
'Truth needs no colour, with his colour fixt;
Beauty no pencil, beauty's truth to lay;
But best is best, if never intermixt'?
Because he needs no praise, wilt thou be dumb?
Excuse not silence so: for't lies in thee
To make him much outlive a gilded tomb,
And to be praised of ages yet to be.
    Then do thy office, Muse; I teach thee how
    To make him seem long hence as he shows now.

102

My love is strengthen'd, though more weak in seeming;
I love not less, though less the show appear:
That love is merchandized whose rich esteeming
The owner's tongue doth publish everywhere.
Our love was new, and then but in the spring,
When I was wont to greet it with my lays;
As Philomel in summer's front doth sing,
And stops her pipe in growth of riper days:
Not that the summer is less pleasant now
Than when her mournful hymns did hush the night,
But that wild music burdens every bough,
And sweets grown common lose their dear delight.
    Therefore, like her, I sometime hold my tongue,
    Because I would not dull you with my song.

103

Alack, what poverty my Muse brings forth,
That having such a scope to show her pride,
The argument, all bare, is of more worth
Than when it hath my added praise beside!
O, blame me not, if I no more can write!
Look in your glass, and there appears a face
That overgoes my blunt invention quite,
Dulling my lines, and doing me disgrace.
Were it not sinful, then, striving to mend,
To mar the subject that before was well?
For to no other pass my verses tend
Than of your graces and your gifts to tell;
    And more, much more, than in my verse can sit,
    Your own glass shows you when you look in it.

104

To me, fair friend, you never can be old,
For as you were when first your eye I eyed,
Such seems your beauty still. Three winters' cold
Have from the forests shook three summers' pride;
Three beauteous springs to yellow autumn turn'd
In process of the seasons have I seen,
Three April perfumes in three hot Junes burn'd,
Since first I saw you fresh, which yet are green.
Ah, yet doth beauty, like a dial-hand,
Steal from his figure, and no pace perceived;
So your sweet hue, which methinks still doth stand,
Hath motion, and mine eye may be deceived:
    For fear of which, hear this, thou age unbred, –
    Ere you were born was beauty's summer dead.

105

Let not my love be call'd idolatry,
Nor my beloved as an idol show,
Since all alike my songs and praises be
To one, of one, still such, and ever so.
Kind is my love to-day, to-morrow kind,
Still constant in a wondrous excellence;
Therefore my verse to constancy confined,
One thing expressing, leaves out difference.
Fair, kind, and true, is all my argument,
Fair, kind, and true, varying to other words;
And in this change is my invention spent,
Three themes in one, which wondrous scope affords.
    Fair, kind, and true, have often lived alone,
    Which three till now never kept seat in one.

106

When in the chronicle of wasted time
I see descriptions of the fairest wights,
And beauty making beautiful old rime
In praise of ladies dead and lovely knights,
Then, in the blazon of sweet beauty's best,
Of hand, of foot, of lip, of eye, of brow,
I see their antique pen would have exprest
Even such a beauty as you master now.
So all their praises are but prophecies
Of this our time, all you prefiguring;
And, for they lookt but with divining eyes,
They had not skill enough your worth to sing:
   For we, which now behold these present days,
   Have eyes to wonder, but lack tongues to praise.

107

Not mine own fears, nor the prophetic soul
Of the wide world dreaming on things to come,
Can yet the lease of my true love control,
Supposed as forfeit to a comfined doom.
The mortal moon hath her eclipse endured,
And the sad augurs mock their own presage;
Incertainties now crown themselves assured,
And peace proclaims olives of endless age.
Now with the drops of this most balmy time
My love looks fresh, and Death to me subscribes,
Since, spite of him, I'll live in this poor rime,
While he insults o'er dull and speechless tribes:
   And thou in this shalt find thy monument,
   When tyrants' crests and tombs of brass are spent.

108

What's in the brain, that ink may character,
Which hath not figured to thee my true spirit?
What's new to speak, what new to register,
That may express my love, or thy dear merit?
Nothing, sweet boy; but yet, like prayers divine.
I must each day say o'er the very same;
Counting no old thing old, thou mine, I thine,
Even as when first I hallow'd thy fair name.
So that eternal love in love's fresh case
Weighs not the dust and injury of age,
Nor gives to necessary wrinkles place,
But makes antiquity for aye his page;
   Finding the first conceit of love there bred,
   Where time and outward form would show it dead.

109

O, never say that I was false of heart,
Though absence seem'd my flame to qualify.
As easy might I from myself depart
As from my soul, which in thy breast doth lie:
That is my home of love: if I have ranged,
Like him that travels I return again,
Just to the time, not with the time exchanged,
So that myself bring water for my stain.
Never believe, though in my nature reign'd
All frailties that besiege all kinds of blood,
That it could so preposterously be stain'd,
To leave for nothing all thy sum of good;
 For nothing this wide universe I call,
 Save thou, my Rose; in it thou art my all.

110

Alas, 'tis true I have gone here and there,
And made myself a motley to the view,
Gored mine own thoughts, sold cheap what is most dear
Made old offences of affections new;
Most true it is that I have lookt on truth
Askance and strangely: but, by all above,
These blenches gave my heart another youth,
And worse essays proved thee my best of love.
Now all is done, have what shall have no end:
Mine appetite I never more will grind
On newer proof, to try an older friend,
A god in love, to whom I am confined.
 Then give me welcome, next my heaven the best,
 Even to thy pure and most most loving breast.

111

O, for my sake do you with Fortune chide,
The guilty goddess of my harmful deeds,
That did not better for my life provide
Than public means which public manners breeds.
Thence comes it that my name receives a brand;
And almost thence my nature is subdued
To what it works in, like the dyer's hand:
Pity me, then, and wish I were renew'd;
Whilst, like a willing patient, I will drink
Potions of eisel 'gainst my strong infection;
No bitterness that I will bitter think,
Nor double penance, to correct correction.
 Pity me, then, dear friend, and I assure ye
 Even that your pity is enough to cure me.

112

Your love and pity doth the impression fill
Which vulgar scandal stampt upon my brow;
For what care I who calls me well or ill,
So you o'er-green my bad, my good allow?
You are my all-the-world, and I must strive
To know my shames and praises from your tongue;
None else to me, nor I to none alive,
That my steel'd sense or changes right or wrong.
In so profound abysm I throw all care
Of others' voices, that my adder's sense
To critic and to flatterer stopped are.
Mark how with my neglect I do dispense:
    You are so strongly in my purpose bred,
    That all the world besides methinks are dead.

113

Since I left you, mine eye is in my mind;
And that which governs me to go about
Doth part his function, and is partly blind,
Seems seeing? but effectually is out;
For it no form delivers to the heart
Of bird, of flower, or shape, which it doth latch:
Of his quick objects hath the mind no part,
Nor his own vision holds what it doth catch;
For if it see the rudest or gentlest sight,
The most sweet favour or deformed'st creature,
The mountain or the sea, the day or night,
The crow or dove, it shapes them to your feature:
    Incapable of more, replete with you,
    My most true mind thus maketh mine untrue.

114

Or whether doth my mind, being crown'd with you,
Drink up the monarch's plague, this flattery?
Or whether shall I say, mine eye saith true,
And that your love taught it this alchemy,
To make of monsters and things indigest
Such cherubins as your sweet self resemble,
Creating every bad a perfect best,
As fast as objects to his beams assemble?
O, 'tis the first; 'tis flatt'ry in my seeing,
And my great mind most kingly drinks it up:
Mine eye well knows what with his gust is greeing,
And to his palate doth prepare the cup:
    If it be poison'd, 'tis the lesser sin
    That mine eye loves it, and doth first begin.

115

Those lines that I before have writ do lie,
Even those that said I could not love you dearer:
Yet then my judgement knew no reason why
My most full flame should afterwards burn clearer.
But reckoning Time, whose million'd accidents
Creep in 'twixt vows, and change decrees of kings,
Tan sacred beauty, blunt the sharp'st intents,
Divert strong minds to the course of alt'ring things;
Alas, why, fearing of Time's tyranny,
Might I not then say, 'Now I love you best,'
When I was certain o'er incertainty,
Crowning the present, doubting of the rest?
    Love is a babe; then might I not say so,
    To give full growth to that which still doth grow.

116

Let me not to the marriage of true minds
Admit impediments. Love is not love
Which alters when it alteration finds,
Or bends with the remover to remove:
O, no! it is an ever-fixed mark,
That looks on tempests, and is never shaken,
It is the star to every wandering bark,
Whose worth's unknown, although his height be taken.
Love's not Time's fool, though rosy lips and cheeks
Within his bending sickle's compass come;
Love alters not with his brief hours and weeks,
But bears it out even to the edge of doom.
    If this be error, and upon me proved,
    I never writ, nor no man ever loved.

117

Accuse me thus: that I have scanted all
Wherein I should your great deserts repay;
Forgot upon your dearest love to call,
Whereto all bonds do tie me day by day;
That I have frequent been with unknown minds,
And given to time your own dear-purchased right;
That I have hoisted sail to all the winds
Which should transport me farthest from your sight.
Book both my wilfulness and errors down,
And on just proof surmise accumulate;
Bring me within the level of your frown,
But shoot not at me in your waken'd hate;
    Since my appeal says I did strive to prove
    The constancy and virtue of your love.

118

Like as, to make our appetites more keen,
With eager compounds we our palate urge;
As, to prevent our maladies unseen,
We sicken to shun sickness when we purge;
Even so, being full of your ne'er-cloying sweetness,
To bitter sauces did I frame my feeding;
And, sick of welfare, found a kind of meetness
To be diseased, ere that there was true needing.
Thus policy in love, t'anticipate
The ills that were not, grew to faults assured,
And brought to medicine a healthful state,
Which, rank of goodness, would by ill be cured:
    But thence I learn, and find the lesson true,
    Drugs poison him that so fell sick of you.

119

What potions have I drunk of Siren tears,
Distill'd from limbecks foul as hell within,
Applying fears to hopes, and hopes to fears,
Still losing when I saw myself to win!
What wretched errors hath my heart committed,
Whilst it hath thought itself so blessed never!
How have mine eyes out of their spheres been fitted
In the distraction of this madding fever!
O benefit of ill! now I find true
That better is by evil still made better;
And ruin'd love, when it is built anew,
Grows fairer than at first, more strong, far greater.
    So I return rebuked to my content,
    And gain by ill thrice more than I have spent.

120

That you were once unkind befriends me now,
And for that sorrow which I then did feel
Needs must I under my transgression bow,
Unless my nerves were brass or hammer'd steel.
For if you were by my unkindness shaken,
As I by yours, y'have past a hell of time;
And I, a tyrant, have no leisure taken
To weigh how once I suffer'd in your crime.
O, that our night of woe might have remember'd
My deepest sense, how hard true sorrow hits,
And soon to you, as you to me then, tender'd
The humble salve which wounded bosoms fits!
    But that, your trespass, now becomes a fee;
    Mine ransoms yours, and yours must ransom me.

121

'Tis better to be vile than vile esteemed,
When not to be receives reproach of being;
And the just pleasure lost, which is so deemed
Not by our feeling, but by others' seeing:
For why should others' false adulterate eyes
Give salutation to my sportive blood?
Or on my frailties why are frailer spies,
Which in their wills count bad what I think good?
No, I am that I am; and they that level
At my abuses reckon up their own:
I may be straight, though they themselves be bevel;
By their rank thoughts my deeds must not be shown
    Unless this general evil they maintain –
    All men are bad, and in their badness reign.

122

Thy gift, thy tables, are within my brain
Full character'd with lasting memory,
Which shall above that idle rank remain,
Beyond all date, even to etemity:
Or at the least, so long as brain and heart
Have faculty by nature to subsist;
Till each to razed oblivion yield his part
Of thee, thy record never can be mist.
That poor retention could not so much hold,
Nor need I tallies thy dear love to score;
Therefore to give them from me was I bold,
To trust those tables that receive thee more:
    To keep an adjunct to remember thee
    Were to import forgetfulness in me.

123

No, Time, thou shalt not boast that I do change:
Thy pyramids built up with newer might
To me are nothing novel, nothing strange;
They are but dressings of a former sight.
Our dates are brief, and therefore we admire
What thou dost foist upon us that is old;
And rather make them born to our desire
Than think that we before have heard them told.
Thy registers and thee I both defy,
Not wondering at the present, nor the past;
For thy records and what we see doth lie,
Made more or less by thy continual haste.
    This I do vow, and this shall ever be,
    I will be true, despite thy scythe and thee.

124

If my dear love were but the child of state,
It might for Fortune's bastard be unfather'd,
As subject to Time's love or to Time's hate,
Weeds among weeds, or flowers with flowers gathered.
No, it was builded far from accident;
It suffers not in smiling pomp, nor falls
Under the blow of thralled discontent,
Whereto the inviting time our fashion calls:
It fears not policy, that heretic,
Which works on leases of short-number'd hours,
But all alone stands hugely politic,
That it nor grows with heat nor drowns with showers.
 To this I witness call the fools of Time,
 Which die for goodness, who have lived for crime.

125

Were't aught to me I bore the canopy,
With my extern the outward honouring,
Or laid great bases for eternity,
Which proves more short than waste or ruining?
Have I not seen dwellers on form and favour
Lose all, and more, by paying too much rent,
For compound sweet foregoing simple savour,
Pitiful thrivers, in their gazing spent?
No, let me be obsequious in thy heart,
And take thou my oblation, poor but free,
Which is not mixt with seconds, knows no art,
But mutual render, only me for thee.
 Hence, thou suborn'd informer! a true soul
 When most impeacht stands least in thy control.

126

O thou, my lovely boy, who in thy power
Dost hold Time's fickle glass, his sickle-hour;
Who hast by waning grown, and therein show'st
Thy lovers withering, as thy sweet self grow'st;
If Nature, sovereign mistress over wrack,
As thou goest onwards, still will pluck thee back.
She keeps thee to this purpose, that her skill
May Time disgrace, and wretched minutes kill.
Yet fear her, O thou minion of her pleasure!
She may detain, but not still keep, her treasure:
 Her audit, though delay'd, answer'd must be,
 And her quietus is to render thee.

127

In the old age black was not counted fair,
Or if it were, it bore not beauty's name;
But now is black beauty's successive heir,
And beauty slander'd with a bastard shame:
For since each hand hath put on nature's power,
Fairing the foul with art's false borrow'd face,
Sweet beauty hath no name, no holy bower,
But is profaned, if not lives in disgrace.
Therefore my mistress' eyes are raven black,
Her eyes so suited, and they mourners seem
At such who, not born fair, no beauty lack,
Slandering creation with a false esteem:
    Yet so they mourn, becoming of their woe,
    That every tongue says beauty should look so.

128

How oft, when thou, my music, music play'st,
Upon that blessed wood whose motion sounds
With thy sweet fingers, when thou gently sway'st
The wiry concord that mine ear confounds,
Do I envy those jacks that nimble leap
To kiss the tender inward of thy hand,
Whilst my poor lips, which should that harvest reap,
At the wood's boldness by thee blushing stand!
To be so tickled, they would change their state
And situation with those dancing chips,
O'er whom thy fingers walk with gentle gait,
Making dead wood more blest than living lips.
    Since saucy jacks so happy are in this,
    Give them thy fingers, me thy lips to kiss.

129

The expense of spirit in a waste of shame
Is lust in action; and till action, lust
Is perjured, murd'rous, bloody, full of blame,
Savage, extreme, rude, cruel, not to trust;
Enjoy'd no sooner but despised straight;
Past reason hunted; and no sooner had,
Past reason hated, as a swallow'd bait,
On purpose laid to make the taker mad:
Mad in pursuit, and in possession so;
Had, having, and in quest to have, extreme;
A bliss in proof and proved, a very woe;
Before, a joy proposed; behind, a dream.
    All this the world well knows; yet none knows well
    To shun the heaven that leads men to this hell.

130

My mistress' eyes are nothing like the sun;
Coral is far more red than her lips red:
If snow be white, why then her breasts are dun;
If hairs be wires, black wires grow on her head.
I have seen roses damaskt, red and white,
But no such roses see I in her cheeks;
And in some perfumes is there more delight
Than in the breath that from my mistress reeks.
I love to hear her speak, yet well I know
That music hath a far more pleasing sound:
I grant I never saw a goddess go;
My mistress, when she walks, treads on the ground.
　　And yet, by heaven, I think my love as rare
　　As any she belied with false compare.

131

Thou art as tyrannous, so as thou art,
As those whose beauties proudly make them cruel;
For well thou know'st to my dear doting heart
Thou art the fairest and most precious jewel.
Yet, in good faith, some say that thee behold,
Thy face hath not the power to make love groan.
To say they err I dare not be so bold,
Although I swear it to myself alone.
And, to be sure that is not false I swear,
A thousand groans, but thinking on thy face,
One on another's neck, do witness bear
Thy black is fairest in my judgement's place.
　　In nothing art thou black save in thy deeds,
　　And thence this slander, as I think, proceeds.

132

Thine eyes I love, and they, as pitying me,
Knowing thy heart torments me with disdain,
Have put on black, and loving mourners be,
Looking with pretty ruth upon my pain.
And truly not the morning sun of heaven
Better becomes the gray cheeks of the east,
Nor that full star that ushers in the even
Doth half that glory to the sober west,
As those two mourning eyes become thy face:
O, let it, then, as well beseem thy heart
To mourn for me, since mourning doth thee grace,
And suit thy pity like in every part.
　　Then will I swear Beauty herself is black,
　　And all they foul that thy complexion lack.

133

Beshrew that heart that makes my heart to groan
For that deep wound it gives my friend and me!
Is't not enough to torture me alone,
But slave to slavery my sweet'st friend must be?
Me from myself thy cruel eye hath taken,
And my next self thou harder hast engrossed:
Of him, myself, and thee, I am forsaken;
A torment thrice threefold thus to be crossed.
Prison my heart in thy steel bosom's ward,
But then my friend's heart let my poor heart bail;
Whoe'er keeps me, let my heart be his guard;
Thou canst not then use rigour in my jail:
    And yet thou wilt; for I, being pent in thee,
    Perforce am thine, and all that is in me.

134

So, now I have confest that he is thine,
And I myself am mortgaged to thy will,
Myself I'll forfeit, so that other mine
Thou wilt restore, to be my comfort still:
But thou wilt not, nor he will not be free,
For thou art covetous, and he is kind;
He learn'd but, surety-like, to write for me,
Under that bond that him as fast doth bind.
The statute of thy beauty thou wilt take,
Thou usurer, that putt'st forth all to use,
And sue a friend came debtor for my sake;
So him I lose through my unkind abuse.
    Him have I lost; thou hast both him and me:
    He pays the whole, and yet am I not free.

135

Whoever hath her wish, thou hast thy *Will*,
And *Will* to boot, and *Will* in overplus;
More than enough am I that vex thee still,
To thy sweet will making addition thus.
Wilt thou, whose will is large and spacious,
Not once vouchsafe to hide my will in thine?
Shall will in others seem right gracious,
And in my will no fair acceptance shine?
The sea, all water, yet receives rain still,
And in abundance addeth to his store;
So thou, being rich in *Will*, add to thy *Will*
One will of mine, to make thy large *Will* more.
    Let no unkind, no fair beseechers kill;
    Think all but one, and me in that one *Will*.

136

If thy soul check thee that I come so near,
Swear to thy blind soul that I was thy *Will,*
And will, thy soul knows, is admitted there;
Thus far for love my love-suit, sweet, fulfil.
Will will fulfil the treasure of thy love,
Ay, fill it full with wills, and my will one.
In things of great receipt with ease we prove
Among a number one is reckon'd none:
Then in the number let me pass untold,
Though in thy store's account I one must be;
For nothing hold me, so it please thee hold
That nothing me, a something, sweet, to thee:
　　Make but my name thy love, and love that still,
　　And then thou lovest me, for my name is *Will.*

137

Thou blind fool, Love, what dost thou to mine eyes,
That they behold, and see not what they see?
They know what beauty is, see where it lies,
Yet what the best is take the worst to be.
If eyes, corrupt by over-partial looks,
Be anchor'd in the bay where all men ride,
Why of eyes' falsehood hast thou forged hooks,
Whereto the judgement of my heart is tied?
Why should my heart think that a several plot
Which my heart knows the wide world's common place?
Or mine eyes seeing this, say this is not,
To put fair truth upon so foul a face?
　　In things right-true my heart and eyes have erred,
　　And to this false plague are they now transferred.

138

When my love swears that she is made of truth,
I do believe her, though I know she lies,
That she might think me some untutor'd youth,
Unlearned in the world's false subtleties.
Thus vainly thinking that she thinks me young,
Although she knows my days are past the best,
Simply I credit her false-speaking tongue:
On both sides thus is simple truth supprest.
But wherefore says she not she is unjust?
And wherefore say not I that I am old?
O, love's best habit is in seeming trust,
And age in love loves not to have years told:
　　Therefore I lie with her and she with me,
　　And in our faults by lies we flatter'd be.

139

O, call not me to justify the wrong
That thy unkindness lays upon my heart;
Wound me not with thine eye, but with thy tongue;
Use power with power, and slay me not by art.
Tell me thou lovest elsewhere; but in my sight,
Dear heart, forbear to glance thine eye aside:
What need'st thou wound with cunning, when thy might
Is more than my o'erprest defence can bide?
Let me excuse thee: ah, my love well knows
Her pretty looks have been mine enemies;
And therefore from my face she turns my foes,
That they elsewhere might dart their injuries:
    Yet do not so; but since I am near slain,
    Kill me outright with looks, and rid my pain.

140

Be wise as thou art cruel; do not press
My tongue-tied patience with too much disdain;
Lest sorrow lend me words, and words express
The manner of my pity-wanting pain.
If I might teach thee wit, better it were,
Though not to love, yet, love, to tell me so;
As testy sick men, when their deaths be near,
No news but health from their physicians know;
For, if I should despair, I should grow mad,
And in my madness might speak ill of thee:
Now this ill-wresting world is grown so bad,
Mad slanderers by mad ears believed be.
    That I may not be so, nor thou belied,
    Bear thine eyes straight, though thy proud heart go wide.

141

In faith, I do not love thee with mine eyes,
For they in thee a thousand errors note;
But 'tis my heart that loves what they despise,
Who, in despite of view, is pleased to dote;
Nor are mine ears with thy tongue's tune delighted;
Nor tender feeling to base touches prone,
Nor taste, nor smell, desire to be invited
To any sensual feast with thee alone:
But my five wits nor my five senses can
Dissuade one foolish heart from serving thee,
Who leaves unsway'd the likeness of a man,
Thy proud heart's slave and vassal wretch to be:
    Only my plague thus far I count my gain,
    That she that makes me sin awards me pain.

142

Love is my sin, and thy dear virtue hate,
Hate of my sin, grounded on sinful loving:
O, but with mine compare thou thine own state,
And thou shalt find it merits not reproving;
Or, if it do, not from those lips of thine,
That have profaned their scarlet ornaments
And seal'd false bonds of love as oft as mine,
Robb'd others' beds' revenues of their rents.
Be it lawful I love thee, as thou lovest those
Whom thine eyes woo as mine importune thee:
Root pity in thy heart, that, when it grows,
Thy pity may deserve to pitied be.
>   If thou dost seek to have what thou dost hide,
>   By self-example mayst thou be denied!

143

Lo, as a careful housewife runs to catch
One of her feather'd creatures broke away,
Sets down her babe, and makes all swift dispatch
In pursuit of the thing she would have stay;
Whilst her neglected child holds her in chase,
Cries to catch her whose busy care is bent
To follow that which flies before her face,
Not prizing her poor infant's discontent:
So runn'st thou after that which flies from thee,
Whilst I thy babe chase thee afar behind;
But if thou catch thy hope, turn back to me,
And play the mother's part, kiss me, be kind:
>   So will I pray that thou mayst have thy *Will*,
>   If thou turn back, and my loud crying still.

144

Two loves I have of comfort and despair,
Which like two spirits do suggest me still:
The better angel is a man right fair,
The worser spirit a woman colour'd ill.
To win me soon to hell, my female evil
Tempteth my better angel from my side,
And would corrupt my saint to be a devil,
Wooing his purity with her foul pride.
And whether that my angel be turn'd fiend
Suspect I may, yet not directly tell;
But being both from me, both to each friend,
I guess one angel in another's hell:
>   Yet this shall I ne'er know, but live in doubt,
>   Till my bad angel fire my good one out.

145

Those lips that Love's own hand did make
Breathed forth the sound that said 'I hate'
To me that languisht for her sake:
But when she saw my woeful state,
Straight in her heart did mercy come,
Chiding that tongue that ever sweet
Was used in giving gentle doom;
And taught it thus anew to greet;
'I hate' she alter'd with an end,
That follow'd it as gentle day
Doth follow night, who like a fiend
From heaven to hell is flown away;
    'I hate' from hate away she threw,
    And saved my life, saying – 'Not you.'

146

Poor soul, the centre of my sinful earth –
My sinful earth these rebel powers array –
Why dost thou pine within and suffer dearth,
Painting thy outward walls so costly gay?
Why so large cost, having so short a lease,
Dost thou upon thy fading mansion spend?
Shall worms, inheritors of this excess,
Eat up thy charge? is this thy body's end?
Then, soul, live thou upon thy servant's loss,
And let that pine to aggravate thy store;
Buy terms divine in selling hours of dross;
Within be fed, without be rich no more:
    So shalt thou feed on Death, that feeds on men,
    And Death once dead, there's no more dying then.

147

My love is as a fever, longing still
For that which longer nurseth the disease;
Feeding on that which doth preserve the ill,
The uncertain sickly appetite to please.
My reason, the physician to my love,
Angry that his prescriptions are not kept,
Hath left me, and I desperate now approve
Desire is death, which physic did except.
Past cure I am, now reason is past care,
And frantic-mad with evermore unrest;
My thoughts and my discourse as madmen's are,
At random from the truth vainly exprest;
    For I have sworn thee fair, and thought thee bright,
    Who art as black as hell, as dark as night.

148

O me, what eyes hath Love put in my head,
Which have no correspondence with true sight!
Or, if they have, where is my judgement fled,
That censures falsely what they see aright?
If that be fair whereon my false eyes dote,
What means the world to say it is not so?
If it be not, then love doth well denote
Love's eye is not so true as all men's: no.
How can it? O, how can Love's eye be true,
That is so vext with watching and with tears?
No marvel, then, though I mistake my view;
The sun itself sees not till heaven clears.
    O cunning Love! with tears thou keep'st me blind,
    Lest eyes well-seeing thy foul faults should find.

149

Canst thou, O cruel! say I love thee not,
When I, against myself, with thee partake?
Do I not think on thee, when I forgot
Am of myself, all tyrant for thy sake?
Who hateth thee that I do call my friend?
On whom frown'st thou that I do fawn upon?
Nay, if thou lour'st on me, do I not spend
Revenge upon myself with present moan?
What merit do I in myself respect,
That is so proud thy service to despise,
When all my best doth worship thy defect,
Commanded by the motion of thine eyes?
    But, love, hate on, for now I know thy mind;
    Those that can see thou lovest, and I am blind.

150

O, from what power hast thou this powerful might
With insufficiency my heart to sway?
To make me give the lie to my true sight,
And swear that brightness doth not grace the day?
Whence hast thou this becoming of things ill,
That in the very refuse of thy deeds
There is such strength and warrantise of skill,
That, in my mind, thy worst all best exceeds?
Who taught thee how to make me love thee more,
The more I hear and see just cause of hate?
O, though I love what others do abhor,
With others thou shouldst not abhor my state:
    If thy unworthiness raised love in me,
    More worthy I to be beloved of thee.

151

Love is too young to know what conscience is;
Yet who knows not conscience is born of love?
Then, gentle cheater, urge not my amiss,
Lest guilty of my faults thy sweet self prove:
For, thou betraying me, I do betray
My nobler part to my gross body's treason;
My soul doth tell my body that he may
Triumph in love; flesh stays no farther reason;
But, rising at thy name, doth point out thee
As his triumphant prize. Proud of this pride,
He is contented thy poor drudge to be,
To stand in thy affairs, fall by thy side.
    No want of conscience hold it that I call
    Her 'love' for whose dear love I rise and fall.

152

In loving thee thou know'st I am forsworn,
But thou art twice forsworn, to me love swearing;
In act thy bed-vow broke, and new faith torn
In vowing new hate after new love bearing.
But why of two oaths' breach do I accuse thee,
When I break twenty? I am perjured most;
For all my vows are oaths but to misuse thee,
And all my honest faith in thee is lost:
For I have sworn deep oaths of thy deep kindness,
Oaths of thy love, thy truth, thy constancy;
And, to enlighten thee, gave eyes to blindness,
Or made them swear against the thing they see;
    For I have sworn thee fair; more perjured I,
    To swear against the truth so foul a lie!

153

Cupid laid by his brand, and fell asleep:
A maid of Dian's this advantage found,
And his love-kindling fire did quickly steep
In a cold valley-fountain of that ground;
Which borrow'd from this holy fire of Love
A dateless lively heat, still to endure,
And grew a seething bath, which yet men prove
Against strange maladies a sovereign cure.
But at my mistress' eye Love's brand new-fired,
The boy for trial needs would touch my breast;
I, sick withal, the help of bath desired,
And thither hied, a sad distemper'd guest,
    But found no cure: the bath for my help lies
    Where Cupid got new fire, – my mistress' eyes.

154

The little Love-god lying once asleep
Laid by his side his heart-inflaming brand,
Whilst many nymphs that vow'd chaste life to keep
Came tripping by; but in her maiden hand
The fairest votary took up that fire
Which many legions of true hearts had warm'd;
And so the general of hot desire
Was sleeping by a virgin hand disarm'd.
This brand she quenched in a cool well by,
Which from Love's fire took heat perpetual,
Growing a bath and healthful remedy
For men diseased; but I, my mistress' thrall,
    Came there for cure, and this by that I prove,
    Love's fire heats water, water cools not love.

THE MYSTERY OF HIS SONNETS

They were published c1609 when he was forty-five, but must have been composed over a period of years.

Many hundreds of scholars have investigated and surmised the reason for their composition and for whom thy were intended.

There's a young man and a black-haired, black-eyed woman!

Conjecture is all very well, but the word-structure, the rhyming and those remarkable 'summing-up' couplets should be enough to transcend the purposes for their composition.

Shakespeare was heavily involved in a theatrical world, with all its sexual and sensual temptations, and may have written these sonnets while contemplating on love. He had already given Anne Hathaway three children by the age of 20, and may have expended his sexual energies in those urgent impulses.

He wrote, acted in and helped to produce 37 great plays in 25 years, and must have lived in a world of his own feverish reading and vivid imagination.

Furthermore, he was a family man. He returned to Stratford regularly on horseback! No helicopters then!

Did his 'craft' come first, his family come second, and the young men and women he met come a very late third?

VENUS AND ADONIS

Vilia miretur vulgus: mihi flavus Apollo
Pocula Castalia plena ministret aqua.

To the Right Honourable Henry Wriothesley, Earl of Southampton, and Baron of Titchfield.

Right Honourable,

I know not how I shall offend in dedicating my unpolisht lines to your Lordship, nor how the world will censure me for choosing so strong a prop to support so weak a burthen: only if your Honour seem but pleased, I account myself highly praised, and vow to take advantage of all idle hours, till I have honour'd you with some graver labour. But if the first heir of my invention prove deform'd, I shall be sorry it had so noble a godfather: and never after ear so barren a land, for fear it yield me still so bad a harvest. I leave it to your honourable survey, and your Honour to your heart's content which I wish may always answer your own wish, and the world's hopeful expectation.

Your Honour's in all duty,

WILLIAM SHAKESPEARE.

Even as the sun with purple-colour'd face
Had ta'en his last leave of the weeping morn,
Rose cheekt Adonis hied him to the chase;
Hunting he loved, but love he laught to scorn:
 Sick-thoughted Venus makes amain unto him,
 And like a bold-faced suitor gins to woo him.

'Thrice-fairer than myself,' thus she began,
'The field's chief flower, sweet above compare,
Stain to all nymphs, more lovely than a man,
More white and red than doves or roses are;
 Nature that made thee, with herself at strife,
 Saith that the world hath ending with thy life.

'Vouchsafe, thou wonder, to alight thy steed,
And rein his proud head to the saddle-bow;
If thou wilt deign this favour, for thy meed
A thousand honey secrets shalt thou know:
 Here come and sit, where never serpent hisses,
 And being set, I'll smother thee with kisses;

'And yet not cloy thy lips with loath'd satiety,
But rather famish them amid their plenty,
Making them red and pale with fresh variety;
Ten kisses short as one, one long as twenty:
A summer's day will seem an hour but short,
Being wasted in such time-beguiling sport.'

With this she seizeth on his sweating palm,
The precedent of pith and livelihood,
And, trembling in her passion, calls it balm,
Earth's sovereign salve to do a goddess good:
Being so enraged, desire doth lend her force
Courageously to pluck him from his horse.

Over one arm the lusty courser's rein,
Under her other was the tender boy,
Who blusht and pouted in a dull disdain,
With leaden appetite, unapt to toy;
She red and hot as coals of glowing fire,
He red for shame, but frosty in desire.

The studded bridle on a lagged bough
Nimbly she fastens: – O, how quick is love! –
The steed is stalled up, and even now
To tie the rider she begins to prove:
Backward she pusht him, as she would be thrust,
And govern'd him in strength, though not in lust.

So soon was she along as he was down,
Each leaning on their elbows and their hips:
Now doth she stroke his cheek, now doth he frown,
And gins to chide, but soon she stops his lips;
And kissing speaks, with lustful language broken,
'If thou wilt chide, thy lips shall never open.'

He burns with bashful shame; she with her tears
Doth quench the maiden burning of his cheeks;
Then with her windy sighs and golden hairs
To fan and blow them dry again she seeks:
He saith she is immodest, blames her miss;
What follows more she murders with a kiss.

Even as an empty eagle, sharp by fast,
Tires with her beak on feathers, flesh, and bone,
Shaking her wings, devouring all in haste,
Till either gorge be stuft, or prey be gone;
Even so she kist his brow, his cheek, his chin,
And where she ends she doth anew begin.

Forced to content, but never to obey,
Panting he lies, and breatheth in her face;
She feedeth on the steam as on a prey,
And calls it heavenly moisture, air of grace;
    Wishing her cheeks were gardens full of flowers,
    So they were dew'd with such distilling showers.

Look how a bird lies tangled in a net,
So fasten'd in her arms Adonis lies;
Pure shame and awed resistance made him fret,
Which bred more beauty in his angry eyes:
    Rain added to a river that is rank
    Perforce will force it overflow the bank.

Still she entreats and prettily entreats,
And to a pretty ear she tunes her tale;
Still is he sullen, still he lours and frets,
'Twixt crimson shame and anger ashy-pale;
    Being red, she loves him best; and being white,
    Her best is better'd with a more delight.

Look how he can, she cannot choose but love;
And by her fair immortal hand she swears,
From his soft bosom never to remove,
'Till he take truce with her contending tears,
    Which long have rain'd, making her cheeks all wet;
    And one sweet kiss shall pay this comptless debt.

Upon this promise did he raise his chin,
Like a dive-dapper peering through a wave,
Who, being lookt on, ducks as quickly in;
So offers he to give what she did crave;
    But when her lips were ready for his pay,
    He winks, and turns his lips another way.

Never did passenger in summer's heat
More thirst for drink than she for this good turn.
Her help she sees, but help she cannot get;
She bathes in water, yet her fire must burn:
    'O, pity,' gan she cry, 'flint-hearted boy!
    'Tis but a kiss I beg; why art thou coy?

'I have been woo'd, as I entreat thee now,
Even by the stern and direful god of war,
Whose sinewy neck in battle ne'er did bow,
Who conquers where he comes in every jar;
    Yet hath he been my captive and my slave,
    And begg'd for that which thou unaskt shalt have.

'Over my altars hath he hung his lance,
His batter'd shield, his uncontrolled crest,
And for my sake hath learnt to sport and dance,
To toy, to wanton, dally, smile, and jest;
    Scorning his churlish drum and ensign red,
    Making my arms his field, his tent my bed.

'Thus he that overruled I overswayed,
Leading him prisoner in a red-rose chain:
Strong-temper'd steel his stronger strength obeyed,
Yet was he servile to my coy disdain.
    'O, be not proud, nor brag not of thy might,
    For mast'ring her that foil'd the god of fight!

'Touch but my lips with those fair lips of thine, –
Though mine be not so fair, yet are they red, –
The kiss shall be thine own as well as mine: –
What see'st thou in the ground? hold up thy head:
    Look in mine eyeballs, there thy beauty lies;
    Then why not lips on lips, since eyes in eyes?

'Art thou ashamed to kiss? then wink again,
And I will wink; so shall the day seem night;
Love keeps his revels where there are but twain;
Be bold to play, our sport is not in sight:
    These blue-vein'd violets whereon we lean
    Never can blab, nor know not what we mean.

'The tender spring upon thy tempting lip
Shows thee unripe; yet mayst thou well be tasted:
Make use of time, let not advantage slip;
Beauty within itself should not be wasted:
    Fair flowers that are not gather'd in their prime
    Rot and consume themselves in little time.

'Were I hard-favour'd, foul, or wrinkled-old,
Ill-nurtured, crooked, churlish, harsh in voice,
O'erworn, despised, rheumatic, and cold,
Thick-sighted, barren, lean, and lacking juice,
    Then mightst thou pause, for then I were not for thee;
    But having no defects, why dost abhor me?

'Thou canst not see one wrinkle in my brow;
Mine eyes are gray, and bright, and quick in turning;
My beauty as the spring doth yearly grow,
My flesh is soft and plump, my marrow burning;
    My smooth moist hand, were it with thy hand felt,
    Would in thy palm dissolve, or seem to melt.

'Bid me discourse, I will enchant thine ear,
Or, like a fairy, trip upon the green,
Or, like a nymph, with long dishevell'd hair,
Dance on the sands, and yet no footing seen:
    Love is a spirit all compact of fire,
    Not gross to sink, but light, and will aspire.

'Witness this primrose bank whereon I lie;
These forceless flowers like sturdy trees support me;
Two strengthless doves will draw me through the sky,
From morn till night, even where I list to sport me:
    Is love so light, sweet boy, and may it be
    That thou should think it heavy unto thee?

'Is thine own heart to thine own face affected?
Can thy right hand seize love upon thy left?
Then woo thyself, be of thyself rejected,
Steal thine own freedom, and complain on theft.
    Narcissus so himself himself forsook,
    And died to kiss his shadow in the brook.

'Torches are made to light, jewels to wear,
Dainties to taste, fresh beauty for the use,
Herbs for their smell, and sappy plants to bear;
Things growing to themselves are growth's abuse:
    Seeds spring from seeds, and beauty breedeth be
    Thou wast begot; to get it is thy duty.

'Upon the earth's increase why shouldst thou feed,
Unless the earth with thy increase be fed?
By law of nature thou art bound to breed,
That thine may live when thou thyself art dead;
    'And so, in spite of death, thou dost survive,
    In that thy likeness still is left alive.'

By this, the love-sick queen began to sweat,
For, where they lay, the shadow had forsook them,
And Titan, tired in the mid-day heat,
With burning eye did hotly overlook them;
    Wishing Adonis had his team to guide
    So he were like him, and by Venus' side.

And now Adonis, with a lazy sprite,
And with a heavy, dark, disliking eye,
His louring brows o'erwhelming his fair sight,
Like misty vapours when they blot the sky, –
    Souring his cheeks, cries, 'Fie, no more of love!
    The sun doth burn my face; I must remove.'

'Ay me,' quoth Venus, 'young, and so unkind?
What bare excuses makest thou to be gone!
I'll sigh celestial breath, whose gentle wind
Shall cool the heat of this descending sun:
    I'll make a shadow for thee of my hairs;
    If they burn too, I'll quench them with my tears.

'The sun that shines from heaven shines but warm,
And, lo, I lie between that sun and thee:
The heat I have from thence doth little harm,
Thine eye darts forth the fire that burneth me;
    And were I not immortal, life were done
    Between this heavenly and earthly sun.

'Art thou obdurate, flinty, hard as steel,
Nay, more than flint, for stone at rain relenteth?
Art thou a woman's son, and canst not feel
What 'tis to love? how want of love tormenteth?
    O, had thy mother borne so hard a mind,
    She had not brought forth thee, but died unkind.

'What am I, that thou shouldst contemn me this?
Or what great danger dwells upon my suit?
What were thy lips the worse for one poor kiss?
Speak, fair; but speak fair words, or else be mute:
    Give me one kiss, I'll give it thee again,
    And one for interest, if thou wilt have twain.

'Fie, lifeless picture, cold and senseless stone,
Well-painted idol, image dull and dead,
Statue contenting but the eye alone,
Thing like a man, but of no woman bred!
    Thou art no man, though of a man's complexion,
    For men will kiss even by their own direction.'

This said, impatience chokes her pleading tongue,
And swelling passion doth provoke a pause;
Red cheeks and fiery eyes blaze forth her wrong;
Being judge in love, she cannot right her cause:
    And now she weeps, and now she fain would speak,
    And now her sobs do her intendments break.

Sometime she shakes her head, and then his hand,
Now gazeth she on him, now on the ground;
Sometime her arms infold him like a band:
She would, he will not in her arms be bound;
    And when from thence he struggles to be gone,
    She locks her lily fingers one in one.

'Fondling,' she saith, 'since I have hemm'd thee here
Within the circuit of this ivory pale,
I'll be a park, and thou shalt be my deer;
Feed where thou wilt, on mountain or in dale:
Graze on my lips; and if those hills be dry,
Stray lower, where the pleasant fountains lie.

'Within this limit is relief enough,
Sweet bottom-grass, and high delightful plain,
Round rising hillocks, brakes obscure and rough,
To shelter thee from tempest and from rain:
Then be my deer, since I am such a park;
No dog shall rouse thee, though a thousand bark.'

At this Adonis smiles as in disdain,
That in each cheek appears a pretty dimple:
Love made those hollows, if himself were slain,
He might be buried in a tomb so simple;
Foreknowing well, if there he came to lie,
Why, there Love lived, and there he could not die.

These lovely caves, these round enchanting pits,
Open'd their mouths to swallow Venus' liking.
Being mad before, how doth she now for wits?
Struck dead at first, what needs a second striking?
Poor queen of love, in thine own law forlorn,
To love a cheek that smiles at thee in scorn!

Now which way shall she turn? what shall she say?
Her words are done, her woes the more increasing;
The time is spent, her object will away,
And from her twining arms doth urge releasing.
'Pity,' she cries, 'some favour, some remorse!'
Away he springs, and hasteth to his horse.

But, lo, from forth a copse that neighbours by,
A breeding jennet, lusty, young, and proud,
Adonis' trampling courser doth espy,
And forth she rushes, snorts, and neighs aloud:
The strong neckt steed, being tied unto a tree,
Breaketh his rein, and to her straight goes he.

Imperiously he leaps, he neighs, he bounds,
And now his woven girths he breaks asunder;
The bearing earth with his hard hoof he wounds,
Whose hollow womb resounds like heaven's thunder;
The iron bit he crusheth 'tween his teeth,
Controlling what he was controlled with.

His ears up-prickt; his braided hanging mane
Upon his compass crest now stand on end;
His nostrils drink the air, and forth again
As from a furnace, vapours doth he send;
    His eye, which scornfully glisters like fire,
    Shows his hot courage and his high desire.

Sometime he trots, as if he told the steps,
With gentle majesty and modest pride;
Anon he rears upright, curvets and leaps,
As who should say, 'Lo, thus my strength is tried;
    And this I do to captivate the eye
    Of the fair breeder that is standing by.'

What recketh he his rider's angry stir,
His flattering 'Holla' or his 'Stand, I say'?
What cares he now for curb or pricking spur?
For rich caparisons or trapping gay?
    He sees his love, and nothing else he sees,
    For nothing else with his proud sight agrees.

Look, when a painter would surpass the life
In limning out a well-proportion'd steed,
His art with nature's workmanship at strife,
As if the dead the living should exceed;
    So did this horse excel a common one
    In shape, in courage, colour, pace, and bone.

Round-hooft, short-jointed, fetlocks shag and long,
Broad breast, full eye, small head, and nostril wide,
High crest, short ears, straight legs, and passing strong,
Thin mane, thick tail, broad buttock, tender hide:
    Look, what a horse should have he did not lack,
    Save a proud rider on so proud a back.

Sometime he scuds far off, and there he stares;
Anon he starts at stirring of a feather;
To bid the wind a base he now prepares,
And whe'r he run or fly they know not whether;
    For through his mane and tail the high wind sing
    Fanning the hairs, who wave like feath'red wings.

He looks upon his love, and neighs unto her;
She answers him, as if she knew his mind:
Being proud, as females are, to see him woo her,
She puts on outward strangeness, seems unkind;
    Spurns at his love, and scorns the heat he feels,
    Beating his kind embracements with her heels.

Then, like a melancholy malcontent,
He vails his tail, that, like a falling plume,
Cool shadow to his melting buttock lent:
He stamps, and bites the poor flies in his fume.
    His love, perceiving how he is enraged,
    Grew kinder, and his fury was assuaged.

His testy master goeth about to take him;
When, lo, the unback breeder, full of fear,
Jealous of catching, swiftly doth forsake him,
With her the horse, and left Adonis there:
    As they were mad, unto the wood they hie them,
    Out-stripping crows that strive to over-fly them.

All swoln with chafing, down Adonis sits,
Banning his boist'rous and unruly beast:
And now the happy season once more fits,
That love-sick Love by pleading may be blest;
    For lovers say, the heart hath treble wrong
    When it is barr'd the aidance of the tongue.

An oven that is stopt, or river stay'd,
Burneth more hotly, swelleth with more rage:
So of concealed sorrow may be said;
Free vent of words love's fire doth assuage;
    But when the heart's attorney once is mute,
    The client breaks, as desperate in his suit.

He sees her coming, and begins to glow,
Even as a dying coal revives with wind,
And with his bonnet hides his angry brow;
Looks on the dull earth with disturbed mind;
    Taking no notice that she is so nigh,
    For all askance he holds her in his eye.

O, what a sight it was, wistly to view
How she came stealing to the wayward boy!
To note the fighting conflict of her hue,
How white and red each other did destroy!
    But now her cheek wax pale, and by and by
    It flasht forth fire, as lightning from the sky.

Now she was just before him as he sat,
And like a lowly lover down she kneels;
With one fair hand she heaveth up his hat,
Her other tender hand his fair cheek feels:
    His tenderer cheek receives her soft hand's print,
    As apt as new-faln snow takes any dint.

O, what a war of looks was then between them!
Her eyes petitioners to his eyes suing;
His eyes saw her eyes as they had not seen them;
Her eyes woo'd still, his eyes disdain'd the wooing:
 And all this dumb-play had his acts made plain
 With tears, which, chorus-like, her eyes did rain.

Full gently now she takes him by the hand,
A lily prison'd in a goal of snow,
Or ivory in an alabaster band;
So white a friend engirts so white a foe:
 This beauteous combat, wilful and unwilling,
 Show'd like two silver doves that sit a-billing.

Once more the engine of her thoughts began:
'O fairest mover on this mortal round,
Would thou wert as I am, and I a man,
My heart all whole as thine, thy heart my wound;
 For one sweet look thy help I would assure thee,
 Though nothing but my body's bane would cure thee.'

'Give me my hand,' saith he; 'why dost thou feel it?'
'Give me my heart,' saith she, 'and thou shalt have it;
O give it me, lest thy hard heart do steel it,
And being steel'd, soft sighs can never grave it:
 Then love's deep groans I never shall regard,
 Because Adonis' heart hath made mine hard.'

'For shame,' he cries, 'let go, and let me go;
My day's delight is past, my horse is gone,
And 'tis your fault I am bereft him so:
I pray you hence, and leave me here alone;
 For all my mind, my thought, my busy care
 Is how to get my palfrey from the mare.'

Thus she replies: 'Thy palfrey, as he should,
Welcomes the warm approach of sweet desire:
Affection is a coal that must be cool'd;
Else, suffer'd, it will set the heart on fire:
 The sea hath bounds, but deep desire hath none;
 Therefore no marvel though thy horse be gone.

'How like a jade he stood, tied to the tree,
Servilely master'd with a leathern rein!
But when he saw his love, his youth's fair fee,
He held such petty bondage in disdain;
 Throwing the base thong from his bending crest,
 Enfranchising his mouth, his back, his breast.

'Who sees true-love in her naked bed,
Teaching the sheets a whiter hue than white,
But, when his glutton eye so full hath fed,
His other agents aim at like delight?
  Who is so faint, that dares not be so bold
  To touch the fire, the weather being cold?

'Let me excuse thy courser, gentle boy;
And learn of him, I heartily beseech thee,
To take advantage on presented joy;
Though I were dumb, yet his proceedings teach thee
  O, learn to love; the lesson is but plain,
  And once made perfect, never lost again.'

'I know not love,' quoth he, 'nor will not know it,
Unless it be a boar, and then I chase it;
'Tis much to borrow, and I will not owe it;
My love to love is love but to disgrace it;
  For I have heard it is a life in death,
  That laughs, and weeps, and all but with a breath.

'Who wears a garment shapeless and unfinisht?
Who plucks the bud before one leaf put forth?
If springing things be any jot diminisht,
They wither in their prime, prove nothing worth:
  The colt that's backt and burden'd being young
  Loseth his pride, and never waxeth strong.

'You hurt my hand with wringing; let us part,
And leave this idle theme, this bootless chat:
Remove your siege from my unyielding heart;
To love's alarms it will not ope the gate:
  Dismiss your vows, your feigned tears, your flatt'ry;
  For where a heart is hard they make no batt'ry.'

'What! canst thou talk?' quoth she, 'hast thou a tongue?
O, would thou hadst not, or I had no hearing!
Thy mermaid's voice hath done me double wrong;
I had my load before, now prest with bearing:
  Melodious discord, heavenly tune harsh-sounding,
  Ear's deep-sweet music, and heart's deep-sore wounding.

'Had I no eyes but ears, my ears would love
That inward beauty and invisible;
Or where I deaf, thy outward parts would move
Each part in me that were but sensible:
  Though neither eyes nor ears, to hear nor see,
  Yet should I be in love by touching thee.

'Say, that the sense of feeling were bereft me,
And that I could not see, nor hear, nor touch,
And nothing but the very smell were left me,
Yet would my love to thee be still as much;
    For from the stillitory of thy face excelling
    Comes breath perfumed, that breedeth love by smelling.

'But, O, what banquet wert thou to the taste,
Being nurse and feeder of the other four!
Would they not wish the feast might ever last,
And bid Suspicion double-lock the door,
    Lest jealousy, that sour unwelcome guest,
    Should, by his stealing in, disturb the feast?'

Once more the ruby-colour'd portal open'd,
Which to his speech did honey passage yield;
Like a red morn, that ever yet betoken'd
Wrack to the seaman, tempest to the field,
    Sorrow to shepherds, woe unto the birds,
    Gusts and foul flaws to herdmen and to herds.

This ill presage advisedly she marketh:
Even as the wind is husht before it raineth,
Or as the wolf doth grin before he barketh,
Or as the berry breaks before it staineth,
    Or like the deadly bullet of a gun,
    His meaning struck her ere his words begun.

And at his look she flatly falleth down,
For looks kill love, and love by looks reviveth:
A smile recures the wounding of a frown;
But blessed bankrout, that by love so thriveth!
    The silly boy, believing she is dead,
    Claps her pale cheek, till clapping makes it red;

And all-amazed brake off his late intent,
For sharply he did think to reprehend her,
Which cunning love did wittily prevent:
Fair fall the wit that can so well defend her!
    For on the grass she lies as she were slain,
    Till his breath breatheth life in her again.

He wrings her nose, he strikes her on the cheeks,
He bends her fingers, holds her pulses hard,
He chafes her lips; a thousand ways he seeks
To mend the hurt that his unkindness marr'd:
    He kisses her; and she, by her good will,
    Will never rise, so he will kiss her still.

The night of sorrow now is turn'd to day:
Her two blue windows faintly she up-heaveth.
Like the fair sun, when in his fresh array
He cheers the morn, and all the earth relieveth:
    And as the bright sun glorifies the sky,
    So is her face illumined with her eye;

Whose beams upon his hairless face are fixt,
As if from thence they borrow'd all their shine.
Were never four such lamps together mixt,
Had not his clouded with his brow's repine;
    But hers, which through the crystal tears gave light,
    Shone like the moon in water seen by night.

'O, where am I?' quoth she; 'in earth or heaven,
Or in the ocean drencht, or in the fire?
What hour is this? or morn or weary even?
Do I delight to die, or life desire?
    But now I lived, and life was death's annoy;
    But now I died, and death was lively joy.

'O, thou didst kill me: kill me once again:
Thy eyes' shrewd tutor, that hard heart of thine,
Hath taught them scornful tricks, and such disdain,
That they have murder'd this poor heart of mine;
    And these mine eyes, true leaders to their queen,
    But for thy piteous lips no more had seen.

'Long may they kiss each other, for this cure!
O, never let their crimson liveries wear!
And as they last, their verdure still endure,
To drive infection from the dangerous year!
    That the star-gazers, having writ on death,
    May say, the plague is banisht by thy breath.

'Pure lips, sweet seals in my soft lips imprinted,
What bargains may I make, still to be sealing?
To sell myself I can be well contented,
So thou wilt buy, and pay, and use good dealing;
    Which purchase if thou make, for fear of slips
    Set thy seal-manual on my wax-red lips.

'A thousand kisses buys my heart from me;
And pay them at thy leisure, one by one.
What is ten hundred touches unto thee?
Are they not quickly told and quickly gone?
    Say, for non-payment that the debt should double,
    Is twenty hundred kisses such a trouble?'

'Fair queen,' quoth he, 'if any love you owe me,
Measure my strangeness with my unripe years:
Before I know myself, seek not to know me;
No fisher but the ungrown fry forbears:
　　The mellow plum doth fall, the green sticks fast,
　　Or being early pluckt is sour to taste.

'Look, the world's comforter, with weary gait,
His day's hot task hath ended in the west;
The owl, night's herald, shrieks; 'tis very late;
The sheep are gone to fold, birds to their nest;
　　And coal black clouds that shadow heaven's light
　　Do summon us to part and bid good night.

'Now let me say "Good night," and so say you;
If you will say so, you shall have a kiss.'
'Good night,' quoth she; and, ere he says 'Adieu,'
The honey fee of parting tender'd is:
　　Her arms do lend his neck a sweet embrace;
　　Incorporate then they seem; face grows to face:

Till, breathless, he disjoin'd, and backward drew
The heavenly moisture, that sweet coral mouth,
Whose precious taste her thirsty lips well knew,
Whereon they surfeit, yet complain on drouth:
　　He with her plenty prest, she faint with dearth,
　　Their lips together glued, fall to the earth.

Now quick desire hath caught the yielding prey,
And glutton-like she feeds, yet never filleth;
Her lips are conquerors, his lips obey,
Paying what ransom the insulter willeth;
　　Whose vulture thought doth pitch the price so high
　　That she will draw his lips' rich treasure dry:

And having felt the sweetness of the spoil,
With blindfold fury she begins to forage;
Her face doth reek and smoke, her blood doth boil,
And careless lust stirs up a desperate courage;
　　Planting oblivion, beating reason back,
　　Forgetting shame's pure blush and honour's wrack.

Hot, faint, and weary with her hard embracing,
Like a wild bird being tamed with too much handling,
Or as the fleet-foot roe that's tired with chasing,
Or like the froward infant still'd with dandling,
　　He now obeys, and now no more resisteth,
　　While she takes all she can, not all she listeth.

What wax so frozen but dissolves with temp'ring,
And yields at last to every light impression?
Things out of hope are compast oft with vent'ring,
Chiefly in love, whose leave exceeds commission:
    Affection faints not like a pale-faced coward,
    But then woos best when most his choice is froward.

When he did frown, O, had she then gave over,
Such nectar from his lips she had not suckt.
Foul words and frowns must not repel a lover;
What though the rose have prickles, yet 'tis pluckt;
    Were beauty under twenty locks kept fast,
    Yet love breaks through and picks them all at last.

For pity now she can no more detain him;
The poor fool prays her that he may depart:
She is resolved no longer to restrain him;
Bids him farewell, and look well to her heart,
    The which, by Cupid's bow she doth protest,
    He carries thence incaged in his breast.

'Sweet boy,' she says, 'this night I'll waste in sorrow,
For my sick heart commands mine eyes to watch.
Tell me, Love's master, shall we meet to-morrow?
Say, shall we? shall we? wilt thou make the match?'
    He tells her, no; to-morrow he intends
    To hunt the boar with certain of his friends.

'The boar!' quoth she; whereat a sudden pale,
Like lawn being spread upon the blushing rose,
Usurps her cheek; she trembles at his tale,
And on his neck her yoking arms she throws:
    She sinketh down, still hanging by his neck,
    He on her belly falls, she on her back.

Now is she in the very lists of love,
Her champion mounted for the hot encounter:
All is imaginary she doth prove,
He will not manage her, although he mount her;
    That worse than Tantalus' is her annoy,
    To clip Elysium, and to lack her joy.

Even so poor birds, deceived with painted grapes
Do surfeit by the eye and pine the maw:
Even so she languisheth in her mishaps
As those poor birds that helpless berries saw,
    The warm effects which she in him finds missing
    She seeks to kindle with continual kissing.

But all in vain; good queen, it will not be:
She hath assay'd as much as may be proved;
Her pleading hath deserved a greater fee;
She's Love, she loves, and yet she is not loved.
    'Fie, fie,' he says, 'you crush me; let me go;
    You have no reason to withhold me so.'

'Thou hadst been gone,' quoth she, 'sweet boy, ere this,
But that thou told'st me thou wouldst hunt the boar.
O, be advised! thou know'st not what it is
With javelin's point a churlish swine to gore,
    Whose tushes never-sheathed he whetteth still,
    Like to a mortal butcher bent to kill.

'On his bow-back he hath a battle set
Of bristly pikes, that ever threat his foes;
His eyes, like glow-worms, shine when he doth fret;
His snout digs sepulchres where'er he goes;
    Being moved, he strikes whate'er is in his way,
    And whom he strikes his crooked tushes slay.

'His brawny sides, with hairy bristles armed,
Are better proof than thy spear's point can enter;
His short thick neck cannot be easily harmed;
Being ireful, on the lion he will venter:
    The thorny brambles and embracing bushes,
    As fearful of him, part; through whom he rushes.

'Alas, he naught esteems that face of thine,
To which Love's eyes pays tributary gazes;
Nor thy soft hands, sweet lips, and crystal eyne,
Whose full perfection all the world amazes;
    But having thee at vantage, – wondrous dread! –
    Would root these beauties as he roots the mead.

'O, let him keep his loathsome cabin still;
Beauty hath naught to do with such foul fiends:
Come not within his danger by thy will;
They that thrive well take counsel of their friends.
    When thou didst name the boar, not to dissemble,
    I fear'd thy fortune, and my joints did tremble.

'Didst thou not mark my face? was it not white?
Saw'st thou not signs of fear lurk in mine eye?
Grew I not faint? and fell I not downright?
Within my bosom, whereon thou dost lie,
    My boding heart pants, beats, and takes no rest,
    But, like an earthquake, shakes thee on my breast.

'For where Love reigns, disturbing Jealousy
Doth call himself Affection's sentinel;
Gives false alarms, suggesteth mutiny,
And in a peaceful hour doth cry "Kill, kill!"
 Distemp'ring gentle Love in his desire,
 As air and water do abate the fire.

'This sour informer, this bate-breeding spy,
This canker that eats up Love's tender spring,
This carry-tale, dissentious Jealousy,
That sometime true news, sometime false doth bring,
 Knocks at my heart, and whispers in mine ear,
 That if I love thee, I thy death should fear:

'And more than so, presenteth to mine eye
The picture of an angry-chafing boar,
Under whose sharp fangs on his back doth lie
An image like thyself, all stain'd with gore;
 Whose blood upon the fresh flowers being shed
 Doth make them droop with grief and hang the head.

'What should I do, seeing thee so indeed,
That tremble at the imagination?
The thought of it doth make my faint heart bleed,
And fear doth teach it divination:
 I prophesy thy death, my living sorrow,
 If thou encounter with the boar to-morrow.

'But if thou needs wilt hunt, be ruled by me;
Uncouple at the timorous flying hare,
Or at the fox which lives by subtlety,
Or at the roe which no encounter dare:
 Pursue these fearful creatures o'er the downs,
 And on thy well-breathed horse keep with thy hounds.

'And when thou hast on foot the purblind hare,
Mark the poor wretch, to overshoot his troubles
How he outruns the wind, and with what care
He cranks and crosses with a thousand doubles:
 The many musets through the which he goes
 Are like a labyrinth to amaze his foes.

'Sometime he runs among a flock of sheep,
To make the cunning hounds mistake their smell,
And sometime where earth-delving conies keep,
To stop the loud pursuers in their yell;
 And sometime sorteth with a herd of deer:
 Danger deviseth shifts; wit waits on fear:

'For there his smell with others being mingled,
The hot scent-snuffing hounds are driven to doubt,
Ceasing their clamorous cry till they have singled
With much ado the cold fault cleanly out;
    Then do they spend their mouths: Echo replies,
    As if another chase were in the skies.

'By this, poor Wat, far off upon a hill,
Stands on his hinder legs with list'ning ear,
To hearken if his foes pursue him still:
Anon their loud alarums he doth hear;
    And now his grief may be compared well
    To one sore sick that hears the passing-bell.

'Then shalt thou see the dew-bedabbled wretch
Turn, and return, indenting with the way;
Each envious brier his weary legs doth scratch,
Each shadow makes him stop, each murmur stay;
    For misery is trodden on by many,
    And being low never relieved by any.

'Lie quietly, and hear a little more;
Nay, do not struggle, for thou shalt not rise:
To make thee hate the hunting of the boar,
Unlike myself thou hear'st me moralize,
    Applying this to that, and so to so;
    For love can comment upon every woe.

'Where did I leave?' 'No matter where,' quoth he;
'Leave me, and then the story aptly ends:
The night is spent.' 'Why, what of that?' quoth she.
'I am,' quoth he, 'expected of my friends;
    And now 'tis dark, and going I shall fall.'
    'In night,' quoth she, 'desire sees best of all.

'But if thou fall, O, then imagine this,
The earth, in love with thee, thy footing trips,
And all is but to rob thee of a kiss.
Rich preys make true-men thieves; so do thy lips
    Make modest Dian cloudy and forlorn,
    Lest she should steal a kiss, and die forsworn.

'Now of this dark night I perceive the reason:
Cynthia for shame obscures her silver shine,
Till forging Nature be condemn'd of treason,
For stealing moulds from heaven that were divine;
    Wherein she framed thee, in high heaven's despite,
    To shame the sun by day, and her by night.

'And therefore hath she bribed the Destinies
To cross the curious workmanship of Nature,
To mingle beauty with infirmities,
And pure perfection with impure defeature,
    Making it subject to the tyranny
    Of mad mischances and much misery;

'As burning fevers, agues pale and faint,
Life-poisoning pestilence, and frenzies wood,
The marrow-eating sickness, whose attaint
Disorder breeds by heating of the blood:
    Surfeits, imposthumes, grief, and damn'd despair,
    Swear Nature's death for framing thee so fair.

'And not the least of all these maladies
But in one minute's fight brings beauty under:
Both favour, savour, hue, and qualities,
Whereat the impartial gazer late did wonder,
    Are on the sudden wasted, thaw'd, and done,
    As mountain snow melts with the midday sun.

'Therefore, despite of fruitless chastity,
Love-lacking vestals, and self-loving nuns,
That on the earth would breed a scarcity
And barren dearth of daughters and of sons,
    Be prodigal: the lamp that burns by night
    Dries up his oil to lend the world his light.

'What is thy body but a swallowing grave,
Seeming to bury that posterity
Which by the rights of time thou needs must have,
If thou destroy them not in dark obscurity?
    If so, the world will hold thee in disdain,
    Sith in thy pride so fair a hope is slain.

'So in thy self thyself art made away;
A mischief worse than civil home-bred strife,
Or theirs whose desperate hands themselves do slay
Or butcher-sire that reaves his son of life.
    Foul-cank'ring rust the hidden treasure frets,
    But gold that's put to use more gold begets.'

'Nay, then,' quoth Adon, 'you will fall again
Into your idle over-handled theme:
The kiss I gave you is bestow'd in vain,
And all in vain you strive against the stream;
    For, by this black-faced night, desire's foul nurse,
    Your treatise makes me like you worse and worse.

'If love have lent you twenty thousand tongues,
And every tongue more moving than your own,
Bewitching like the wanton mermaid's songs,
Yet from mine ear the tempting tune is blown;
    For know, my heart stands armed in mine ear,
    And will not let a false sound enter there;

'Lest the deceiving harmony should run
Into the quiet closure of my breast;
And then my little heart were quite undone,
In his bedchamber to be barr'd of rest.
    No, lady, no; my heart longs not to groan,
    But soundly sleeps, while now it sleeps alone.

'What have you urged that I cannot reprove?
The path is smooth that leadeth on to danger:
I hate not love, but your device in love,
That lends embracements unto every stranger.
    You do it for increase: O strange excuse,
    When reason is the bawd to lust's abuse!

'Call it not love, for Love to heaven is fled,
Since sweating Lust on earth usurpt his name;
Under whose simple semblance he hath fed
Upon fresh beauty, blotting it with blame;
    Which the hot tyrant stains and soon bereaves,
    As caterpillars do the tender leaves.

'Love comforteth like sunshine after rain,
But Lust's effect is tempest after sun;
Love's gentle spring doth always fresh remain,
Lust's winter comes ere summer half be done;
    Love surfeits not, Lust like a glutton dies;
    Love is all truth, Lust full of forged lies.

'More I could tell, but more I dare not say;
The text is old, the orator too green.
Therefore, in sadness, now I will away;
My face is full of shame, my heart of teen:
    Mine ears, that to your wanton talk attended,
    Do burn themselves for having so offended.'

With this, he breaketh from the sweet embrace
Of those fair arms which bound him to her breast,
And homeward through the dark laund runs apace;
Leaves Love upon her back deeply distrest.
    Look, how a bright star shooteth from the sky,
    So glides he in the night from Venus' eye;

Which after him she darts, as one on shore
Gazing upon a late-embarked friend,
Till the wild waves will have him see no more,
Whose ridges with the meeting clouds contend:
    So did the merciless and pitchy night
    Fold-in the object that did feed her sight.

Whereat amazed, as one that unaware
Hath dropt a precious jewel in the flood,
Or stonisht as night-wanderers often are,
Their light blown out in some mistrustful wood;
    Even so confounded in the dark she lay,
    Having lost the fair discovery of her way.

And now she beats her heart, whereat it groans,
That all the neighbour caves, as seeming troubled,
Make verbal repetition of her moans;
Passion on passion deeply is redoubled:
    'Ay me!' she cries, and twenty times, 'Woe, woe!'
    And twenty echoes twenty times cry so.

She, marking them, begins a wailing note,
And sings extemporally a woeful ditty;
How love makes young men thrall, and old men dote;
How love is wise in folly, foolish-witty:
    Her heavy anthem still concludes in woe,
    And still the choir of echoes answer so.

Her song was tedious, and outwore the night,
For lovers' hours are long, though seeming short:
If pleased themselves, others, they think, delight
In such-like circumstance, with such-like sport:
    Their copious stories, oftentimes begun,
    End without audience, and are never done.

For who hath she to spend the night withal,
But idle sounds resembling parasits;
Like shrill-tongued tapsters answering every call,
Soothing the humour of fantastic wits?
    She says ' 'Tis so:' they answer all, ' 'Tis so;'
    And would say after her, if she said 'No.'

Lo, here the gentle lark, weary of rest,
From his moist cabinet mounts up on high,
And wakes the morning, from whose silver breast
The sun ariseth in his majesty;
    Who doth the world so gloriously behold,
    That cedar-tops and hills seem burnisht gold.

Venus salutes him with this fair good-morrow:
'O thou clear god, and patron of all light,
From whom each lamp and shining star doth borrow
The beauteous influence that makes him bright,
    There lives a son, that suckt an earthly mother,
    May lend thee light, as thou dost lend to other.'

This said, she hasteth to a myrtle grove,
Musing the morning is so much o'erworn,
And yet she hears no tidings of her love:
She hearkens for his hounds and for his horn:
    Anon she hears them chant it lustily,
    And all in haste she coasteth to the cry.

And as she runs, the bushes in the way
Some catch her by the neck, some kiss her face,
Some twined about her thigh to make her stay:
She wildly breaketh from their strict embrace,
    Like a milch doe, whose swelling dugs do ache,
    Hasting to feed her fawn hid in some brake.

By this, she hears the hounds are at a bay:
Whereat she starts, like one that spies an adder
Wreathed up in fatal folds just in his way,
The fear whereof doth make him shake and shudder;
    Even so the timorous yelping of the hounds
    Appals her senses and her spirit confounds.

For now she knows it is no gentle chase,
But the blunt boar, rough bear, or lion proud,
Because the cry remaineth in one place,
Where fearfully the dogs exclaim aloud:
    Finding their enemy to be so curst,
    They all strain court'sy who shall cope him first.

This dismal cry rings sadly in her ear,
Through which it enters to surprise her heart;
Who, overcome by doubt and bloodless fear,
With cold-pale weakness numbs each feeling part:
    Like soldiers, when their captain once doth yield,
    They basely fly, and dare not stay the field.

Thus stands she in a trembling ecstasy;
Till, cheering up her senses all dismay'd,
She tells them 'tis a causeless fantasy,
And childish error, that they are afraid;
    Bids them leave quaking, bids them fear no more:
    And with that word she spied the hunted boar;

Whose frothy mouth, bepainted all with red,
Like milk and blood being mingled both togither,
A second fear through all her sinews spread,
Which madly hurries her she knows not whither:
    This way she runs, and now she will no further,
    But back retires to rate the boar for murther.

A thousand spleens bear her a thousand ways;
She treads the path that she untreads again;
Her more than haste is mated with delays,
Like the proceedings of a drunken brain,
    Full of respects, yet naught at all respecting;
    In hand with all things, naught at all effecting.

Here kennell'd in a brake she finds a hound,
And asks the weary caitiff for his master;
And there another licking of his wound,
'Gainst venom'd sores the only sovereign plaster;
    And here she meets another sadly scowling,
    To whom she speaks, and he replies with howling.

When he hath ceased his ill-resounding noise,
Another flap-mouth'd mourner, black and grim,
Against the welkin volleys out his voice;
Another and another answer him,
    Clapping their proud tails to the ground below,
    Shaking their scratcht ears, bleeding as they go.

Look how the world's poor people are amazed
At apparitions, signs, and prodigies,
Whereon with fearful eyes they long have gazed,
Infusing them with dreadful prophecies;
    So she at these sad signs draws up her breath,
    And, sighing it again, exclaims on Death.

'Hard-favour'd tyrant, ugly, meagre, lean,
Hateful divorce of love.' – thus chides she Death, –
'Grim-grinning ghost, earth's worm, what dost thou mean
To stifle beauty and to steal his breath,
    Who when he lived, his breath and beauty set
    Gloss on the rose, smell to the violet?

'If he be dead, – O no, it cannot be,
Seeing his beauty, thou shouldst strike at it; –
O yes, it may; thou hast no eyes to see,
But hatefully at random dost thou hit.
    Thy mark is feeble age; but thy false dart
    Mistakes that aim, and cleaves an infant's heart.

'Hadst thou but bid beware, then he had spoke,
And, hearing him, thy power had lost his power.
The Destinies will curse thee for this stroke;
They bid thee crop a weed, thou pluck'st a flower:
>   Love's golden arrow at him should have fled,
>   And not Death's ebon dart, to strike him dead.

'Dost thou drink tears, that thou provokest such weeping?
What may a heavy groan advantage thee?
Why hast thou cast into eternal sleeping
Those eyes that taught all other eyes to see?
>   Now Nature cares not for thy mortal vigour,
>   Since her best work is ruin'd with thy rigour.'

Here overcome, as one full of despair,
She vail'd her eyelids, who, like sluices, stopt
The crystal tide that from her two cheeks fair
In the sweet channel of her bosom dropt;
>   But through the flood-gates breaks the silver rain,
>   And with his strong course opens them again.

O, how her eyes and tears did lend and borrow!
Her eye seen in the tears, tears in her eye;
Both crystals, where they view'd each other's sorrow, –
Sorrow that friendly sighs sought still to dry;
>   But like a stormy day, now wind, now rain,
>   Sighs dry her cheeks, tears make them wet again.

Variable passions throng her constant woe,
As striving who should best become her grief;
All entertain'd, each passion labours so,
That every present sorrow seemeth chief,
>   But none is best: then join they all together,
>   Like many clouds consulting for foul weather.

By this, far off she hears some huntsman hollo;
A nurse's song ne'er pleased her babe so well:
The dire imagination she did follow
This sound of hope doth labour to expel;
>   For now reviving joy bids her rejoice,
>   And flatters her it is Adonis' voice.

Whereat her tears began to turn their tide,
Being prison'd in her eye like pearls in glass;
Yet sometimes falls an orient drop beside,
Which her cheek melts, as scorning it should pass,
>   To wash the foul face of the sluttish ground,
>   Who is but drunken when she seemeth drown'd.

O hard-believing love, how strange it seems
Not to believe, and yet too credulous!
Thy weal and woe are both of them extremes;
Despair and hope makes thee ridiculous:
> The one doth flatter thee in thoughts unlikely,
> In likely thoughts the other kills thee quickly.

Now she unweaves the web that she hath wrought;
Adonis lives, and Death is not to blame;
It was not she that call'd him all to-naught:
Now she adds honours to his hateful name;
> She clepes him king of graves, and grave for kings,
> Imperious supreme of all mortal things.

'No, no,' quoth she, 'sweet Death, I did but jest;
Yet pardon me I felt a kind of fear
Whenas I met the boar, that bloody beast
Which knows no pity, but is still severe:
> Then, gentle shadow, – truth I must confess, –
> I rail'd on thee, fearing my love's decease.

'Tis not my fault: the boar provoked my tongue;
Be wreakt on him, invisible commander;
'Tis he, foul creature, that hath done thee wrong;
I did but act, he's author of thy slander:
> Grief hath two tongues; and never woman yet
> Could rule them both without ten women's wit.'

Thus hoping that Adonis is alive,
Her rash suspect she doth extenuate;
And that his beauty may the better thrive,
With Death she humbly doth insinuate;
> Tells him of trophies, statues, tombs, and stories
> His victories, his triumphs, and his glories.

'O Jove,' quoth she, 'how much a fool was I
To be of such a weak and silly mind
To wail his death who lives, and must not die
Till mutual overthrow of mortal kind!
> For he being dead, with him is beauty slain,
> And, beauty dead, black chaos comes again.

'Fie, fie, fond love, thou art as full of fear
As one with treasure laden hemm'd with thieves;
Trifles, unwitnessed with eye or ear,
Thy coward heart with false bethinking grieves.'
> Even at this word she hears a merry horn,
> Whereat she leaps that was but late forlorn.

As falcons to the lure, away she flies;
The grass stoops not, she treads on it so light;
And in her haste unfortunately spies
The foul boar's conquest on her fair delight;
Which seen, her eyes, as murder'd with the view,
Like stars ashamed of day, themselves withdrew;

Or as the snail, whose tender horns being hit,
Shrinks backward in his shelly cave with pain,
And there, all smother'd up, in shade doth sit,
Long after fearing to creep forth again;
So at his bloody view her eyes are fled
Into the deep-dark cabins of her head:

Where they resign their office and their light
To the disposing of her troubled brain;
Who bids them still consort with ugly night,
And never wound the heart with looks again;
Who, like a king perplexed in his throne,
By their suggestion gives a deadly groan.

Whereat each tributary subject quakes;
As when the wind, imprison'd in the ground,
Struggling for passage, earth's foundation shakes,
Which with cold terror doth men's minds confound.
This mutiny each part doth so surprise,
That from their dark beds once more leap her eyes;

And, being open'd, threw unwilling light
Upon the wide wound that the boar had trencht
In his soft flank; whose wonted lily white
With purple tears, that his wound wept, was drencht:
No flower was nigh, no grass, herb, leaf, or weed,
But stole his blood, and seem'd with him to bleed.

This solemn sympathy poor Venus noteth;
Over one shoulder doth she hang her head:
Dumbly she passions, franticly she doteth;
She thinks he could not die, he is not dead:
Her voice is stopt, her joints forget to bow;
Her eyes are mad that they have wept till now.

Upon his hurt she looks so steadfastly,
That her sight dazzling makes the wound seem three;
And then she reprehends her mangling eye,
That makes more gashes where no breach should be:
His face seems twain, each several limb is doubled;
For oft the eye mistakes, the brain being troubled.

'My tongue cannot express my grief for one,
And yet,' quoth she, 'behold two Adons dead!
My sighs are blown away, my salt tears gone,
Mine eyes are turn'd to fire, my heart to lead:
    Heavy heart's lead, melt at mine eyes' red fire!
    So shall I die by drops of hot desire.

'Alas, poor world, what treasure hast thou lost!
What face remains alive that's worth the viewing?
Whose tongue is music now? what canst thou boast
Of things long since, or any thing ensuing?
    The flowers are sweet, their colours fresh and trim;
    But true-sweet beauty lived and died with him.

'Bonnet nor veil henceforth no creature wear!
Nor sun nor wind will ever strive to kiss you:
Having no fair to lose, you need not fear;
The sun doth scorn you, and the wind doth hiss you:
    But when Adonis lived, sun and sharp air
    Lurkt like two thieves, to rob him of his fair:

'And therefore would he put his bonnet on,
Under whose brim the gaudy sun would peep;
The wind would blow it off, and, being gone,
Play with his locks: then would Adonis weep;
    And straight, in pity of his tender years,
    They both would strive who first should dry his tears.

'To see his face the lion walkt along
Behind some hedge, because he would not fear him;
To recreate himself when he hath sung,
The tiger would be tame, and gently hear him;
    If he had spoke, the wolf would leave his prey,
    And never fright the silly lamb that day.

'When he beheld his shadow in the brook,
The fishes spread on it their golden gills;
When he was by, the birds such pleasure took,
That some would sing, some other in their bills
    Would bring him mulberries and ripe-red cherries;
    He fed them with his sight, they him with berries.

'But this foul, grim, and urchin-snouted boar,
Whose downward eye still looketh for a grave,
Ne'er saw the beauteous livery that he wore;
Witness the entertainment that he gave:
    If he did see his face, why then I know
    He thought to kiss him, and hath kill'd him so.

'Tis true, 'tis true; thus was Adonis slain:
He ran upon the boar with his sharp spear,
Who did not whet his teeth at him again,
But by a kiss thought to persuade him there,
    And nuzzling in his flank, the loving swine
    Sheathed, unaware, the tusk in his soft groin.

'Had I been tooth'd like him, I must confess,
With kissing him I should have kill'd him first;
But he is dead, and never did he bless
My youth with his; the more am I accurst.'
    With this, she falleth in the place she stood,
    And stains her face with his congealed blood.

She looks upon his lips, and they are pale;
She takes him by the hand, and that is cold;
She whispers in his ears a heavy tale,
As if they heard the woeful words she told;
    She lifts the coffer-lids that close his eyes,
    Where, lo, two lamps, burnt out, in darkness lies;

Two glasses, where herself herself beheld
A thousand times, and now no more reflect;
Their virtue lost, wherein they late excell'd,
And every beauty robb'd of his effect:
    'Wonder of time,' quoth she, 'this is my spite,
    That, thou being dead, the day should yet be light.

'Since thou art dead, lo, here I prophesy
Sorrow on love hereafter shall attend:
It shall be waited on with jealousy,
Find sweet beginning, but unsavoury end;
    Ne'er settled equally, but high or low;
    That all love's pleasure shall not match his woe.

'It shall be fickle, false, and full of fraud;
Bud and be blasted in a breathing-while;
The bottom poison, and the top o'erstraw'd
With sweets that shall the truest sight beguile:
    The strongest body shall it make most weak,
    Strike the wise dumb, and teach the fool to speak.

'It shall be sparing and too full of riot,
Teaching decrepit age to tread the measures;
The staring ruffian shall it keep in quiet,
Pluck down the rich, enrich the poor with treasures;
    It shall be raging-mad and silly-mild,
    Make the young old, the old become a child.

'It shall suspect where is no cause of fear;
It shall not fear where it should most mistrust;
It shall be merciful and too severe,
And most deceiving when it seems most just;
 Perverse it shall be where it shows most toward,
 Put fear to valour, courage to the coward.

'It shall be cause of war and dire events,
And set dissension 'twixt the son and sire;
Subject and servile to all discontents,
As dry combustious matter is to fire:
 Sith in his prime Death doth my love destroy,
 They that love best their loves shall not enjoy.'

By this, the boy that by her side lay kill'd
Was melted like a vapour from her sight;
And in his blood, that on the ground lay spill'd,
A purple flower sprung up, chequer'd with white,
 Resembling well his pale cheeks, and the blood
 Which in round drops upon their whiteness stood.

She bows her head the new-sprung flower to smell,
Comparing it to her Adonis' breath;
And says within her bosom it shall dwell,
Since he himself is reft from her by Death:
 She crops the stalk, and in the breach appears
 Green-dropping sap, which she compares to tears.

'Poor flower,' quoth she, 'this was thy father's guise, –
Sweet issue of a more sweet-smelling sire, –
For every little grief to wet his eyes:
To grow unto himself was his desire,
 And so 'tis thine; but know, it is as good
 To wither in my breast as in his blood.

'Here was thy father's bed, here in my breast;
Thou art the next of blood, and 'tis thy right:
Lo, in this hollow cradle take thy rest,
My throbbing heart shall rock thee day and night:
 There shall not be one minute in an hour
 Wherein I will not kiss my sweet love's flower.'

Thus weary of the world away she hies,
And yokes her silver doves; by whose swift aid
Their mistress, mounted, through the empty skies
In her light chariot quickly is convey'd;
 Holding their course to Paphos, where their queen
 Means to immure herself and not be seen.

LUCRECE

To the Right Honourable Henry Wriothesley,
Earl of Southampton, and Baron of Titchfield

The love I dedicate to your Lordship is without end; whereof this
pamphlet, without beginning, is but a superfluous moiety. The warrant I
have of your honourable disposition, not the worth of my untutor'd lines,
makes it assured of acceptance. What I have done is yours; what I have
to do is yours; being part in all I have, devoted yours. Were my worth
greater, my duty would show greater; meantime, as it is, it is bound to
your Lordship, to whom I wish long life, still lengthen'd with all
happiness.

Your Lordship's in all duty,

WILLIAM SHAKESPEARE.

THE ARGUMENT.

Lucius Tarquinius (for his excessive pride surnamed Superbus), after he had
caused his own father-in-law Servius Tullius to be cruelly murder'd, and,
contrary to the Roman laws and customs, not requiring or staying for the
people's suffrages, had possest himself of the kingdom, went, accompanied
with his sons and other noblemen of Rome, to besiege Ardea. During which
siege the principal men of the army meeting one evening at the tent of
Sextus Tarquinius, the king's son, in their discourses after supper every one
commended the virtues of his own wife; among whom Collatinus extoll'd the
incomparable chastity of his wife Lucretia. In that pleasant humour they all
posted to Rome; and intending, by their secret and sudden arrival, to make
trial of that which every one had before avoucht, only Collatinus finds his
wife, though it were late in the night, spinning amongst her maids: the other
ladies were all found dancing and revelling, or in several disports.
Whereupon the noblemen yielded Collatinus the victory, and his wife the
fame. At that time Sextus Tarquinius being inflamed with Lucrece' beauty, yet
smothering his passions for the present, departed with the rest back to the
camp; from whence he shortly after privily withdrew himself, and was
(according to his estate) royally entertain'd and lodged by Lucrece at
Collatium. The same night he treacherously stealeth into her chamber,
violently ravisht her, and early in the morning speedeth away. Lucrece, in this
lamentable plight, hastily dispatcheth messengers, one to Rome for her
father, another to the camp for Collatine. They came, the one accompanied
with Junius Brutus, the other with Publius Valerius; and finding Lucrece
attired in mourning habit, demanded the cause of her sorrow. She, first
taking an oath of them for her revenge, reveal'd the actor, and whole manner
of his dealing, and withal suddenly stabb'd herself. Which done, with one
consent they all vow'd to root out the whole hated family of the Tarquins; and
bearing the dead body to Rome, Brutus acquainted the people with the doer
and manner of the vile deed, with a bitter invective against the tyranny of the
king: wherewith the people were so moved, that with one consent and a
general acclamation the Tarquins were all exiled, and the state government
changed from kings to consuls.

From the besieged Ardea all in post,
Borne by the trustless wings of false desire,
Lust-breathed Tarquin leaves the Roman host,
And to Collatium bears the lightless fire
Which, in pale embers hid, lurks to aspire
    And girdle with embracing flames the waist
    Of Collatine's fair love, Lucrece the chaste.

Haply that name of 'chaste' unhap'ly set
This bateless edge on his keen appetite;
When Collatine unwisely did not let
To praise the clear unmatched red and white
Which triumpht in that sky of his delight,
    Where mortal stars, as bright as heaven's beauties,
    With pure aspects did him peculiar duties.

For he the night before, in Tarquin's tent,
Unlockt the treasure of his happy state;
What priceless wealth the heavens had him lent
In the possession of his beauteous mate;
Reckoning his fortune at such high-proud rate,
    That kings might be espoused to more fame,
    But king nor peer to such a peerless dame.

O happiness enjoy'd but of a few!
And, if possest, as soon decay'd and done
As is the morning's silver-melting dew
Against the golden splendour of the sun!
An expired date, cancell'd ere well begun:
    Honour and beauty, in the owner's arms,
    Are weakly fortrest from a world of harms.

Beauty itself doth of itself persuade
The eyes of men without an orator;
What needeth, then, apologies be made,
To set forth that which is so singular?
Or why is Collatine the publisher
    Of that rich jewel he should keep unknown
    From thievish ears, because it is his own?

Perchance his boast of Lucrece' sovereignty
Suggested this proud issue of a king;
For by our ears our hearts oft tainted be:
Perchance that envy of so rich a thing,
Braving compare, disdainfully did sting
    His high-pitcht thoughts, that meaner men should vaunt
    That golden hap which their superiors want.

But some untimely thought did instigate
His all-too-timeless speed, if none of those:
His honour, his affairs, his friends, his state,
Neglected all, with swift intent he goes
To quench the coal which in his liver glows.
    O rash-false heat, wrapt in repentant cold,
    Thy hasty spring still blasts, and ne'er grows old!

When at Collatium this false lord arrived,
Well was he welcomed by the Roman dame,
Within whose face Beauty and Virtue strived
Which of them both should underprop her fame:
When Virtue bragg'd, Beauty would blush for shame;
    When Beauty boasted blushes, in despite
    Virtue would stain that o'er with silver white.

But Beauty, in that white intituled,
From Venus' doves doth challenge that fair field:
Then Virtue claims from Beauty Beauty's red,
Which Virtue gave the golden age to gild
Their silver cheeks, and call'd it then their shield;
    Teaching them thus to use it in the fight, –
    When shame assail'd, the red should fence the white.

This heraldry in Lucrece' face was seen,
Argued by Beauty's red and Virtue's white:
Of either's colour was the other queen,
Proving from world's minority their right:
Yet their ambition makes them still to fight;
    The sovereignty of either being so great,
    That oft they interchange each other's seat.

This silent war of lilies and of roses,
Which Tarquin view'd in her fair face's field,
In their pure ranks his traitor eye encloses;
Where, lest between them both it should be kill'd,
The coward captive vanquished doth yield
    To those two armies that would let him go,
    Rather than triumph in so false a foe.

Now thinks he that her husband's shallow tongue, –
The niggard prodigal that praised her so, –
In that high task hath done her beauty wrong,
Which far exceeds his barren skill to show:
Therefore that praise which Collatine doth owe
    Enchanted Tarquin answers with surmise,
    In silent wonder of still-gazing eyes.

This earthly saint, adored by this devil,
Little suspecteth the false worshipper;
For unstain'd thoughts do seldom dream on evil
Birds never limed no secret bushes fear:
So guiltless she securely gives good cheer
    And reverend welcome to her princely guest,
    Whose inward ill no outward harm exprest:

For that he colour'd with his high estate,
Hiding base sin in plaits of majesty;
That nothing in him seem'd inordinate,
Save sometime too much wonder of his eye,
Which, having all, all could not satisfy;
    But, poorly rich, so wanteth in his store,
    That, cloy'd with much, he pineth still for more.

But she, that never coped with stranger eyes,
Could pick no meaning from their parling looks,
Nor read the subtle-shining secrecies
Writ in the glassy margents of such books:
She toucht no unknown baits, nor fear'd no hooks;
    Nor could she moralize his wanton sight,
    More than his eyes were open'd to the light.

He stories to her ears her husband's fame,
Won in the fields of fruitful Italy;
And decks with praises Collatine's high name,
Made glorious by his manly chivalry
With bruised arms and wreaths of victory:
    Her joy with heaved-up hand she doth express,
    And, wordless, so greets heaven for his success.

Far from the purpose of his coming thither,
He makes excuses for his being there:
No cloudy show of stormy blustering weather
Doth yet in his fair welkin once appear;
Till sable Night, mother of dread and fear,
    Upon the world dim darkness doth display,
    And in her vaulty prison stows the Day.

For then is Tarquin brought unto his bed,
Intending weariness with heavy sprite;
For, after supper, long he questioned
With modest Lucrece, and wore out the night:
Now leaden slumber with life's strength doth fight;
    And every one to rest themselves betake,
    Save thieves, and cares, and troubled minds, that wake.

As one of which doth Tarquin lie revolving
The sundry dangers of his will's obtaining;
Yet ever to obtain his will resolving,
Though weak-built hopes persuade him to abstaining:
Despair to gain doth traffic oft for gaining;
  And when great treasure is the meed proposed,
  Though death be adjunct, there's no death supposed.

Those that much covet are with gain so fond,
That what they have not, that which they possess,
They scatter and unloose it from their bond,
And so, by hoping more, they have but less;
Or, gaining more, the profit of excess
  Is but to surfeit, and such griefs sustain,
  That they prove bankrout in this poor-rich gain.

The aim of all is but to nurse the life
With honour, wealth, and ease, in waning age;
And in this aim there is such thwarting strife,
That one for all, or all for one we gage;
As life for honour in fell battle's rage;
  Honour for wealth; and oft that wealth doth cost
  The death of all, and all together lost.

So that in vent'ring ill we leave to be
The things we are for that which we expect;
And this ambitious foul infirmity,
In having much, torments us with defect
Of that we have: so then we do neglect
  The thing we have; and, all for want of wit,
  Make something nothing by augmenting it.

Such hazard now must doting Tarquin make,
Pawning his honour to obtain his lust;
And for himself himself he must forsake:
Then where is truth, if there be no self-trust?
When shall he think to find a stranger just,
  When he himself himself confounds, betrays
  To slanderous tongues and wretched hateful days?

Now stole upon the time the dead of night,
When heavy sleep had closed up mortal eyes:
No comfortable star did lend his light,
No noise but owls' and wolves' death-boding cries;
Now serves the season that they may surprise
  The silly lambs: pure thoughts are dead and still,
  While lust and murder wakes to stain and kill.

And now this lustful lord leapt from his bed,
Throwing his mantle rudely o'er his arm;
Is madly tost between desire and dread;
Th'one sweetly flatters, th'other feareth harm;
But honest fear, bewitcht with lust's foul charm,
    Doth too-too oft betake him to retire,
    Beaten away by brain-sick rude desire.

His falchion on a flint he softly smiteth,
That from the cold stone sparks of fire do fly;
Whereat a waxen torch forthwith he lighteth,
Which must be lode-star to his lustful eye;
And to the flame thus speaks advisedly,
    'As from this cold flint I enforced this fire,
    So Lucrece must I force to my desire.'

Here pale with fear he doth premeditate
The dangers of his loathsome enterprise,
And in his inward mind he doth debate
What following sorrow may on this arise:
Then looking scornfully, he doth despise
    His naked armour of still-slaughter'd lust,
    And justly thus controls his thoughts unjust:

'Fair torch, burn out thy light, and lend it not
To darken her whose light excelleth thine:
And die, unhallow'd thoughts, before you blot
With your uncleanness that which is divine;
Offer pure incense to so pure a shrine:
    Let fair humanity abhor the deed
    That spots and stains love's modest snow-white weed.

'O shame to knighthood and to shining arms!
O foul dishonour to my household's grave!
O impious act, including all foul harms!
A martial man to be soft fancy's slave!
True valour still a true respect should have;
    Then my digression is so vile, so base,
    That it will live engraven in my face.

'Yea, though I die, the scandal will survive,
And be an eye-sore in my golden coat;
Some loathsome dash the herald will contrive,
To cipher me how fondly I did dote;
That my posterity, shamed with the note,
    Shall curse my bones, and hold it for no sin
    To wish that I their father had not bin.

'What win I, if I gain the thing I seek?
A dream, a breath, a froth of fleeting joy.
Who buys a minute's mirth to wail a week?
Or sells eternity to get a toy?
For one sweet grape who will the vine destroy?
    Or what fond begger, but to touch the crown,
    Would with the sceptre straight be strucken down?

'If Collatinus dream of my intent,
Will he not wake, and in a desperate rage
Post hither, this vile purpose to prevent?
This siege that hath engirt his marriage,
This blur to youth, this sorrow to the sage,
    This dying virtue, this surviving shame,
    Whose crime will bear an ever-during blame?

'O, what excuse can my invention make,
When thou shalt charge me with so black a deed?
Will not my tongue be mute, my frail joints shake,
Mine eyes forgo their light, my false heart bleed?
The guilt being great, the fear doth still exceed;
    And extreme fear can neither fight nor fly,
    But coward-like with trembling terror die.

'Had Collatinus kill'd my son or sire,
Or lain in ambush to betray my life,
Or were he not my dear friend, this desire
Might have excuse to work upon his wife,
As in revenge or quittal of such strife:
    But as he is my kinsman, my dear friend,
    The shame and fault finds no excuse nor end.

'Shameful it is; – ay, if the fact be known:
Hateful it is; – there is no hate in loving:
I'll beg her love; – but she is not her own:
The worst is but denial and reproving:
My will is strong, past reason's weak removing.
    Who fears a sentence or an old man's saw
    Shall by a painted cloth be kept in awe.'

Thus, graceless, holds he disputation
'Tween frozen conscience and hot burning will,
And with good thoughts makes dispensation,
Urging the worser sense for vantage still;
Which in a moment doth confound and kill
    All pure effects, and doth so far proceed,
    That what is vile shows like a virtuous deed.

Quoth he, 'She took me kindly by the hand,
And gazed for tidings in my eager eyes,
Fearing some hard news from the warlike band,
Where her beloved Collatinus lies.
O, how her fear did make her colour rise!
    First red as roses that on lawn we lay,
    Then white as lawn, the roses took away.

'And how her hand, in my hand being lockt,
Forced it to tremble with her loyal fear!
Which struck her sad, and then it faster rockt,
Until her husband's welfare she did hear;
Whereat she smiled with so sweet a cheer,
    That had Narcissus seen her as she stood,
    Self-love had never drown'd him in the flood.

'Why hunt I, then, for colour or excuses?
All orators are dumb when beauty pleadeth;
Poor wretches have remorse in poor abuses;
Love thrives not in the heart that shadows dreadeth:
Affection is my captain, and he leadeth;
    And when his gaudy banner is display'd,
    The coward fights, and will not be dismay'd.

'Then, childish fear avaunt! debating die!
Respect and reason wait on wrinkled age!
My heart shall never countermand mine eye:
Sad pause and deep regard beseems the sage;
My part is youth, and beats these from the stage:
    Desire my pilot is, beauty my prize;
    Then who fears sinking where such treasure lies?'

As corn o'ergrown by weeds, so heedful fear
Is almost choked by unresisted lust.
Away he steals with open listening ear,
Full of foul hope and full of fond mistrust;
Both which, as servitors to the unjust,
    So cross him with their opposite persuasion,
    That now he vows a league, and now invasion.

Within his thought her heavenly image sits,
And in the self-same seat sits Collatine:
That eye which looks on her confounds his wits;
That eye which him beholds, as more divine,
Unto a view so false will not incline;
    But with a pure appeal seeks to the heart,
    Which once corrupted takes the worser part;

And therein heartens up his servile powers,
Who, flatter'd by their leader's jocund show,
Stuff up his lust, as minutes fill up hours;
And as their captain, so their pride doth grow,
Paying more slavish tribute than they owe.
 By reprobate desire thus madly led,
 The Roman lord marcheth to Lucrece' bed.

The locks between her chamber and his will,
Each one by him enforced, retires his ward;
But, as they open, they all rate his ill,
Which drives the creeping thief to some regard:
The threshold grates the door to have him heard;
 Night-wandering weasels shriek to see him there;
 They fright him, yet he still pursues his fear.

As each unwilling portal yields him way,
Through little vents and crannies of the place
The wind wars with his torch to make him stay,
And blows the smoke of it into his face,
Extinguishing his conduct in this case;
 But his hot heart, which fond desire doth scorch,
 Puffs forth another wind that fires the torch:

And being lighted, by the light he spies
Lucretia's glove, wherein her needle sticks:
He takes it from the rushes where it lies,
And griping it, the, needle his finger pricks;
As who should say, 'This glove to wanton tricks
 Is not inured; return again in haste;
 Thou see'st our mistress' ornaments are chaste.'

But all these poor forbiddings could not stay him;
He in the worst sense consters their denial:
The doors, the wind, the glove, that did delay him,
He takes for accidental things of trial;
Or as those bars which stop the hourly dial,
 Who with a lingering stay his course doth let,
 Till every minute pays the hour his debt.

'So, so,' quoth he, 'these lets attend the time,
Like little frosts that sometime threat the spring,
To add a more rejoicing to the prime,
And give the sneaped birds more cause to sing.
Pain pays the income of each precious thing;
 Huge rocks, high winds, strong pirates, shelves and sands,
 The merchant fears, ere rich at home he lands.'

Now is he come unto the chamber-door
That shuts him from the heaven of his thought,
Which with a yielding latch, and with no more,
Hath barr'd him from the blessed thing he sought.
So from himself impiety hath wrought,
    That for his prey to pray he doth begin,
    As if the heavens should countenance his sin.

But in the midst of his unfruitful prayer,
Having solicited th'eternal power
That his foul thoughts might compass his fair fair,
And they would stand auspicious to the hour,
Even there he starts: – quoth he, 'I must deflower:
    The powers to whom I pray abhor this fact,
    How can they, then, assist me in the act?

'Then Love and Fortune be my gods, my guide!
My will is backt with resolution:
Thoughts are but dreams till their effects be tried;
The blackest sin is clear'd with absolution;
Against love's fire fear's frost hath dissolution.
    The eye of heaven is out, and misty night
    Covers the shame that follows sweet delight.'

This said, his guilty hand pluckt up the latch,
And with his knee the door he opens wide.
The dove sleeps fast that this night-owl will catch:
Thus treason works ere traitors be espied.
Who sees the lurking serpent steps aside;
    But she, sound sleeping, fearing no such thing,
    Lies at the mercy of his mortal sting.

Into the chamber wickedly he stalks,
And gazeth on her yet-unstained bed.
The curtains being close, about he walks,
Rolling his greedy eyeballs in his head:
By their high treason is his heart misled;
    Which gives the watch-word to his hand full soon
    To draw the cloud that hides the silver moon.

Look, as the fair and fiery-pointed sun,
Rushing from forth a cloud, bereaves our sight;
Even so, the curtain drawn, his eyes begun
To wink, being blinded with a greater light:
Whether it is that she reflects so bright,
    That dazzleth them, or else some shame supposed;
    But blind they are, and keep themselves enclosed.

O, had they in that darksome prison died!
Then had they seen the period of their ill;
Then Collatine again, by Lucrece' side,
In his clear bed might have reposed still:
But they must ope, this blessed league to kill;
    And holy-thoughted Lucrece to their sight
    Must sell her joy, her life, her world's delight.

Her lily hand her rosy cheek lies under,
Cozening the pillow of a lawful kiss;
Who, therefore angry, seems to part in sunder,
Swelling on either side to want his bliss;
Between whose hills her head entombed is:
    Where, like a virtuous monument, she lies,
    To be admired of lewd unhallow'd eyes.

Without the bed her other fair hand was,
On the green coverlet; whose perfect white
Show'd like an April daisy on the grass,
With pearly sweat, resembling dew of night.
Her eyes, like marigolds, had sheathed their light,
    And canopied in darkness sweetly lay,
    Till they might open to adorn the day.

Her hair, like golden threads, play'd with her breath;
O modest wantons! wanton modesty!
Showing life's triumph in the map of death,
And death's dim look in life's mortality:
Each in her sleep themselves so beautify,
    As if between them twain there were no strife,
    But that life lived in death, and death in life.

Her breasts, like ivory globes circled with blue,
A pair of maiden worlds unconquered,
Save of their lord no bearing yoke they knew,
And him by oath they truly honoured.
These worlds in Tarquin new ambition bred;
    Who, like a foul usurper, went about
    From this fair throne to heave the owner out.

What could he see but mightily he noted?
What did he note but strongly he desired?
What he beheld, on that he firmly doted,
And in his will his wilful eye he tired.
With more than admiration he admired
    Her azure veins, her alabaster skin,
    Her coral lips, her snow-white dimpled chin.

As the grim lion fawneth o'er his prey,
Sharp hunger by the conquest satisfied,
So o'er this sleeping soul doth Tarquin stay,
His rage of lust by gazing qualified;
Slackt, not supprest; for standing by her side,
    His eye, which late this mutiny restrains,
    Unto a greater uproar tempts his veins:

And they, like straggling slaves for pillage fighting,
Obdurate vassals fell exploits effecting,
In bloody death and ravishment delighting,
Nor children's tears nor mothers' groans respecting,
Swell in their pride, the onset still expecting:
    Anon his beating heart, alarum striking,
    Gives the hot charge, and bids them do their liking.

His drumming heart cheers up his burning eye,
His eye commends the leading to his hand;
His hand, as proud of such a dignity,
Smoking with pride, marcht on to make his stand
On her bare breast, the heart of all her land;
    Whose ranks of blue veins, as his hand did scale,
    Left their round turrets destitute and pale.

They, mustering to the quiet cabinet
Where their dear governess and lady lies,
Do tell her she is dreadfully beset,
And fright her with confusion of their cries:
She, much amazed, breaks ope her lockt-up eyes,
    Who, peeping forth this tumult to behold,
    Are by his flaming torch dimm'd and controll'd.

Imagine her as one in dead of night
From forth dull sleep by dreadful fancy waking,
That thinks she hath beheld some ghastly sprite,
Whose grim aspect sets every joint a-shaking;
What terror 'tis! but she, in worser taking,
    From sleep disturbed, heedfully doth view
    The sight which makes supposed terror true.

Wrapt and confounded in a thousand fears,
Like to a new-kill'd bird she trembling lies;
She dares not look; yet, winking, there appears
Quick-shifting antics, ugly in her eyes:
Such shadows are the weak brain's forgeries;
    Who, angry that the eyes fly from their lights,
    In darkness daunts them with more dreadful sights.

His hand, that yet remains upon her breast, –
Rude ram, to batter such an ivory wall! –
May feel her heart – poor citizen! – distrest,
Wounding itself to death, rise up and fall,
Beating her bulk, that his hand shakes withal.
 This moves in him more rage, and lesser pity,
 To make the breach, and enter this sweet city.

First, like a trumpet, doth his tongue begin
To sound a parley to his heartless foe;
Who o'er the white sheet peers her whiter chin,
The reason of this rash alarm to know,
Which he by dumb demeanour seeks to show;
 But she with vehement prayers urgeth still
 Under what colour he commits this ill.

Thus he replies: 'The colour in thy face –
That even for anger makes the lily pale,
And the red rose blush at her own disgrace –
Shall plead for me and tell my loving tale:
Under that colour am I come to scale
 Thy never-conquer'd fort: the fault is thine,
 For those thine eyes betray thee unto mine.

'Thus I forestall thee, if thou mean to chide:
Thy beauty hath ensnared thee to this night,
Where thou with patience must my will abide;
My will that marks thee for my earth's delight,
Which I to conquer sought with all my might;
 But as reproof and reason beat it dead,
 By thy bright beauty was it newly bred.

'I see what crosses my attempt will bring;
I know what thorns the growing rose defends;
I think the honey guarded with a sting;
All this beforehand counsel comprehends:
But will is deaf, and hears no heedful friends;
 Only he hath an eye to gaze on beauty,
 And dotes on what he looks, 'gainst law or duty.

'I have debated, even in my soul,
What wrong, what shame, what sorrow I shall breed;
But nothing can affection's course control,
Or stop the headlong fury of his speed.
I know repentant tears ensue the deed,
 Reproach, disdain, and deadly enmity;
 Yet strive I to embrace mine infamy.'

This said, he shakes aloft his Roman blade,
Which, like a falcon towering in the skies,
Coucheth the fowl below with his wings' shade,
Whose crooked beak threats if he mount he dies:
So under his insulting falchion lies
    Harmless Lucretia, marking what he tells
    With trembling fear, as fowl hear falcon's bells.

'Lucrece,' quoth he, 'this night I must enjoy thee:
If thou deny, then force must work my way,
For in thy bed I purpose to destroy thee:
That done, some worthless slave of thine I'll slay,
To kill thine honour with thy life's decay;
    And in thy dead arms do I mean to place him,
    Swearing I slew him, seeing thee embrace him.

'So thy surviving husband shall remain
The scornful mark of every open eye;
Thy kinsmen hang their heads at this disdain,
Thy issue blurr'd with nameless bastardy:
And thou, the author of their obloquy,
    Shalt have thy trespass cited up in rimes,
    And sung by children in succeeding times.

'But if thou yield, I rest thy secret friend:
The fault unknown is as a thought unacted;
A little harm done to a great good end
For lawful policy remains enacted.
The poisonous simple sometime is compacted
    In a pure compound; being so applied,
    His venom in effect is purified.

'Then, for thy husband and thy children's sake,
Tender my suit: bequeath not to their lot
The shame that from them no device can take,
The blemish that will never be forgot;
Worse than a slavish wipe or birth-hour's blot:
    For marks descried in men's nativity
    Are nature's faults, not their own infamy.'

Here with a cockatrice' dead-killing eye
He rouseth up himself, and makes a pause;
While she, the picture of true piety,
Like a white hind under the gripe's sharp claws,
Pleads, in a wilderness where are no laws,
    To the rough beast that knows no gentle right,
    Nor aught obeys but his foul appetite.

But when a black-faced cloud the world doth threat,
In his dim mist the aspiring mountains hiding,
From earth's dark womb some gentle gust doth get,
Which blows these pitchy vapours from their biding,
Hindering their present fall by this dividing;
    So his unhallow'd haste her words delays,
    And moody Pluto winks while Orpheus plays.

Yet, foul night-waking cat, he doth but dally,
While in his hold-fast foot the weak mouse panteth:
Her sad behaviour feeds his vulture folly,
A swallowing gulf that even in plenty wanteth:
His ear her prayers admits, but his heart granteth
    No penetrable entrance to her plaining:
    Tears harden lust, though marble wear with raining.

Her pity-pleading eyes are sadly fixed
In the remorseless wrinkles of his face;
Her modest eloquence with sighs is mixed,
Which to her oratory adds more grace.
She puts the period often from his place;
    And midst the sentence so her accent breaks,
    That twice she doth begin ere once she speaks.

She conjures him by high almighty Jove,
By knighthood, gentry, and sweet friendship's oath,
By her untimely tears, her husband's love,
By holy human law, and common troth,
By heaven and earth, and all the power of both,
    That to his borrow'd bed he make retire,
    And stoop to honour, not to foul desire.

Quoth she, 'Reward not hospitality
With such black payment as thou hast pretended;
Mud not the fountain that gave drink to thee;
Mar not the thing that cannot be amended;
End thy ill aim before thy shoot be ended;
    He is no woodman that doth bend his bow
    To strike a poor unseasonable doe.

'My husband is thy friend, – for his sake spare me;
Thyself art mighty, – for thine own sake leave me;
Myself a weakling, – do not, then, ensnare me;
Thou look'st not like deceit, – do not deceive me.
My sighs, like whirlwinds, labour hence to heave thee:
    If ever man were moved with woman's moans,
    Be moved with my tears, my sighs, my groans:

'All which together, like a troubled ocean,
Beat at thy rocky and wrack-threatening heart,
To soften it with their continual motion;
For stones dissolved to water do convert.
O, if no harder than a stone thou art,
    Melt at my tears, and be compassionate!
    Soft pity enters at an iron gate.

'In Tarquin's likeness I did entertain thee:
Hast thou put on his shape to do him shame?
To all the host of heaven I complain me,
Thou wrong'st his honour, wound'st his princely name.
Thou art not what thou seem'st; and if the same,
    Thou seem'st not what thou art, a god, a king;
    For kings like gods should govern every thing.

'How will thy shame be seeded in thine age,
When thus thy vices bud before thy spring!
If in thy hope thou darest do such outrage,
What darest thou not when once thou art a king?
O, be remember'd, no outrageous thing
    From vassal actors can be wiped away;
    Then kings' misdeeds cannot be hid in clay.

'This deed will make thee only loved for fear;
But happy monarchs still are fear'd for love:
With foul offenders thou perforce must bear,
When they in thee the like offences prove:
If but for fear of this, thy will remove;
    For princes are the glass, the school, the book,
    Where subjects' eyes do learn, do read, do look.

'And wilt thou be the school where Lust shall learn?
Must he in thee read lectures of such shame?
Wilt thou be glass wherein it shall discern
Authority for sin, warrant for blame,
To privilege dishonour in thy name?
    Thou back'st reproach against long-living laud,
    And makest fair reputation but a bawd.

'Hast thou command? by him that gave it thee,
From a pure heart command thy rebel will:
Draw not thy sword to guard iniquity,
For it was lent thee all that brood to kill.
Thy princely office how canst thou fulfil,
    When, pattern'd by thy fault, foul Sin may say,
    He learnt to sin, and thou didst teach the way?

'Think but how vile a spectacle it were,
To view thy present trespass in another.
Men's faults do seldom to themselves appear;
Their own transgressions partially they smother:
This guilt would seem death-worthy in thy brother.
    O, how are they wrapt in with infamies
    That from their own misdeeds askance their eyes!

'To thee, to thee, my heaved-up hands appeal,
Not to seducing lust, thy rash relier:
I sue for exiled majesty's repeal;
Let him return, and flattering thoughts retire:
His true respect will prison false desire,
    And wipe the dim mist from thy doting eyne,
    That thou.shalt see thy state, and pity mine.'

'Have done,' quoth he: 'my uncontrolled tide
Turns not, but swells the higher by this let.
Small lights are soon blown out, huge fires abide,
And with the wind in greater fury fret:
The petty streams that pay a daily debt
    To their salt sovereign, with their fresh falls' haste
    Add to his flow, but alter not his taste.'

'Thou art,' quoth she, 'a sea, a sovereign king;
And, lo, there falls into thy boundless flood
Black lust, dishonour, shame, misgoverning,
Who seek to stain the ocean of thy blood.
If all these petty ills shall change thy good,
    Thy sea within a puddle's womb is hearsed,
    And not the puddle in thy sea dispersed.

'So shall these slaves be king, and thou their slave;
Thou nobly base, they basely dignified;
Thou their fair life, and they thy fouler grave:
Thou loathed in their shame, they in thy pride:
The lesser thing should not the greater hide;
    The cedar stoops not to the base shrub's foot,
    But low shrubs wither at the cedar's root.

'So let thy thoughts, low vassals to thy state'
'No more,' quoth he; 'by heaven, I will not hear thee:
Yield to my love; if not, enforced hate,
Instead of love's coy touch, shall rudely tear thee;
That done, despitefully I mean to bear thee
    Unto the base bed of some rascal groom,
    To be thy partner in this shameful doom.'

This said, he sets his foot upon the light,
For light and lust are deadly enemies:
Shame folded up in blind-concealing night,
When most unseen, then most doth tyrannize.
The wolf hath seized his prey, the poor lamb cries;
    Till with her own white fleece her voice controll'd
    Entombs her outcry in her lips' sweet fold:

For with the nightly linen that she wears
He pens her piteous clamours in her head;
Cooling his hot face in the chastest tears
That ever modest eyes with sorrow shed.
O, that prone lust should stain so pure a bed!
    The spots whereof could weeping purify,
    Her tears should drop on them perpetually.

But she hath lost a dearer thing than life,
And he hath won what he would lose again:
This forced league doth force a further strife;
This momentary joy breeds months of pain;
This hot desire converts to cold disdain:
    Pure Chastity is rifled of her store,
    And Lust, the thief, far poorer than before.

Look, as the full-fed hound or gorged hawk,
Unapt for tender smell or speedy flight,
Make slow pursuit, or altogether balk
The prey wherein by nature they delight;
So surfeit-taking Tarquin fares this night:
    His taste delicious, in digestion souring,
    Devours his will, that lived by foul devouring.

O, deeper sin than bottomless conceit
Can comprehend in still imagination!
Drunken Desire must vomit his receipt,
Ere he can see his own abomination.
While Lust is in his pride, no exclamation
    Can curb his heat, or rein his rash desire,
    Till, like a jade, Self-will himself doth tire.

And then with lank and lean discolour'd cheek,
With heavy eye, knit brow, and strengthless pace,
Feeble Desire, all recreant, poor, and meek,
Like to a bankrout beggar wails his case:
The flesh being proud, Desire doth fight with Grace,
    For there it revels; and when that decays,
    The guilty rebel for remission prays.

So fares it with this faultful lord of Rome,
Who this accomplishment so hotly chased;
For now against himself he sounds this doom, –
That through the length of times he stands disgraced:
Besides, his soul's fair temple is defaced;
　　To whose weak ruins muster troops of cares,
　　To ask the spotted princess how she fares.

She says, her subjects with foul insurrection
Have batter'd down her consecrated wall,
And by their mortal fault brought in subjection
Her immortality, and made her thrall
To living death and pain perpetual:
　　Which in her prescience she controlled still,
　　But her foresight could not forestall their will.

Even in this thought through the dark night he stealeth,
A captive victor that hath lost in gain;
Bearing away the wound that nothing healeth,
The scar that will, despite of cure, remain;
Leaving his spoil perplext in greater pain.
　　She bears the load of lust he left behind,
　　And he the burthen of a guilty mind.

He like a thievish dog creeps sadly thence;
She like a wearied lamb lies panting there;
He scowls, and hates himself for his offence;
She, desperate, with her nails her flesh doth tear;
He faintly flies, sweating with guilty fear;
　　She stays, exclaiming on the direful night;
　　He runs, and chides his vanisht, loathed delight.

He thence departs a heavy convertite;
She there remains a hopeless castaway;
He in his speed looks for the morning light;
She prays she never may behold the day,
'For day,' quoth she, 'night's scapes doth open lay,
　　And my true eyes have never practised how
　　To cloak offences with a cunning brow.

'They think not but that every eye can see
The same disgrace which they themselves behold;
And therefore would they still in darkness be,
To have their unseen sin remain untold;
For they their guilt with weeping will unfold,
　　And grave, like water that doth eat in steel,
　　Upon my cheeks what helpless shame I feel.'

Here she exclaims against repose and rest,
And bids her eyes hereafter still be blind.
She wakes her heart by beating on her breast,
And bids it leap from thence, where it may find
Some purer chest to close so pure a mind.
    Frantic with grief thus breathes she forth her spite
    Against the unseen secrecy of night:

'O comfort-killing Night, image of hell!
Dim register and notary of shame!
Black stage for tragedies and murders fell!
Vast sin-concealing chaos! nurse of blame!
Blind muffled bawd! dark harbour for defame!
    Grim cave of death! whispering conspirator
    With close-tongued treason and the ravisher!

'O hateful, vaporous, and foggy Night!
Since thou art guilty of my cureless crime,
Muster thy mists to meet the eastern light,
Make war against proportion'd course of time;
Or if thou wilt permit the sun to climb
    His wonted height, yet ere he go to bed,
    Knit poisonous clouds about his golden head.

'With rotten damps ravish the morning air;
Let their exhaled unwholesome breaths make sick
The life of purity, the supreme fair,
Ere he arrive his weary noon-tide prick;
And let thy misty vapours march so thick,
    That in their smoky ranks his smother'd light
    May set at noon, and make perpetual night.

'Were Tarquin Night, as he is but Night's child,
The silver-shining queen he would distain;
Her twinkling handmaids too, by him defiled
Through Night's black bosom should not peep again:
So should I have co-partners in my pain;
    And fellowship in woe doth woe assuage,
    As palmers' chat makes short their pilgrimage.

'Where now I have no one to blush with me',
To cross their arms, and hang their heads with mine,
To mask their brows, and hide their infamy;
But I alone alone must sit and pine,
Seasoning the earth with showers of silver brine,
    Mingling my talk with tears, my grief with groans,
    Poor wasting monuments of lasting moans.

'O Night, thou furnace of foul-reeking smoke,
Let not the jealous Day behold that face
Which underneath thy black all-hiding cloak
Immodestly lies martyr'd with disgrace!
Keep still possession of thy gloomy place,
    That all the faults which in thy reign are made
    May likewise be sepulchred in thy shade!

'Make me not object to the tell-tale Day!
The light will show, character'd in my brow,
The story of sweet chastity's decay,
The impious breach of holy wedlock vow:
Yea, the illiterate, that know not how
    To cipher what is writ in learned books,
    Will quote my loathsome trespass in my looks.

'The nurse, to still her child, will tell my story,
And fright her crying babe with Tarquin's name;
The orator, to deck his oratory,
Will couple my reproach to Tarquin's shame;
Feast-finding minstrels, tuning my defame,
    Will tie the hearers to attend each line,
    How Tarquin wronged me, I Collatine.

'Let my good name, that senseless reputation,
For Collatine's dear love be kept unspotted:
If that be made a theme for disputation,
The branches of another root are rotted,
And undeserved reproach to him allotted
    That is as clear from this attaint of mine
    As I, ere this, was pure to Collatine.

'O unseen shame! invisible disgrace!
O unfelt sore! crest-wounding, private scar!
Reproach is stampt in Collatinus' face,
And Tarquin's eye may read the mot afar,
How he in peace is wounded, not in war.
    Alas, how many bear such shameful blows,
    Which not themselves, but he that gives them knows!

'If, Collatine, thine honour lay in me,
From me by strong assault, it is bereft.
My honey lost, and I, a drone-like bee,
Have no perfection of my summer left,
But robb'd and ransackt by injurious theft:
    In thy weak hive a wandering wasp hath crept,
    And suckt the honey which thy chaste bee kept.

'Yet am I guilty of thy honour's wrack, –
Yet for thy honour did I entertain him;
Coming from thee, I could not put him back,
For it had been dishonour to disdain him:
Besides, of weariness he did complain him,
    And talkt of virtue: – O unlookt-for evil,
    When virtue is profaned in such a devil!

'Why should the worm intrude the maiden bud?
Or hateful cuckoos hatch in sparrows' nests?
Or toads infect fair founts with venom mud?
Or tyrant folly lurk in gentle breasts?
Or kings be breakers of their own behests?
    But no perfection is so absolute,
    That some impurity doth not pollute.

'The aged man that coffers-up his gold
Is plagued with cramps and gouts and painful fits;
And scarce hath eyes his treasure to behold,
And like still-pining Tantalus he sits,
And useless barns the harvest of his wits;
    Having no other pleasure of his gain
    But torment that it cannot cure his pain.

'So then he hath it when he cannot use it,
And leaves it to be master'd by his young;
Who in their pride do presently abuse it:
Their father was too weak, and they too strong,
To hold their cursed-blessed fortune long.
    The sweets we wish for turn, to loathed sours
    Even in the moment that we call them ours.

'Unruly blasts wait on the tender spring;
Unwholesome weeds take root with precious flowers:
The adder hisses where the sweet birds sing:
What virtue breeds iniquity devours:
We have no good that we can say is ours,
    But ill-annexed Opportunity
    Or kills his life or else his quality.

'O Opportunity, thy guilt is great!
'Tis thou that executest the traitor's treason;
Thou sett'st the wolf where he the lamb may get;
Whoever plots the sin, thou point'st the season;
'Tis thou that spurn'st at right, at law, at reason;
    And in thy shady cell, where none may spy him,
    Sits Sin, to seize the souls that wander by him.

'Thou makest the vestal violate her oath;
Thou blow'st the file when temperance is thaw'd;
Thou smother'st honesty, thou murder'st troth;
Thou foul abettor! thou notorious bawd!
Thou plantest scandal, and displacest laud:
    Thou ravisher, thou traitor, thou false thief,
    Thy honey turns to gall, thy joy to grief!

'Thy secret pleasure turns to open shame,
Thy private feasting to a public fast,
Thy smoothing titles to a ragged name,
Thy sugar'd tongue to bitter wormwood taste:
Thy violent vanities can never last.
    How comes it, then, vile Opportunity,
    Being so bad, such numbers seek for thee?

'When wilt thou be the humble suppliant's friend,
And bring him where his suit may be obtained?
When wilt thou sort an hour great strifes to end?
Or free that soul which wretchedness hath chained?
Give physic to the sick, ease to the pained?
    The poor, lame, blind, halt, creep, cry out for thee;
    But they ne'er meet with Opportunity.

'The patient dies while the physician sleeps;
The orphan pines while the oppressor feeds;
Justice is feasting while the widow weeps;
Advice is sporting while infection breeds:
Thou grant'st no time for charitable deeds:
    Wrath, envy, treason, rape, and murder's rages,
    Thy heinous hours wait on them as their pages.

'When Truth and Virtue have to do with thee,
A thousand crosses keep them from thy aid:
They buy thy help; but Sin ne'er gives a fee,
He gratis comes; and thou art well appaid
As well to hear as grant what he hath said.
    My Collatine would else have come to me
    When Tarquin did, but he was stay'd by thee.

'Guilty thou art of murder and of theft,
Guilty of perjury and subornation,
Guilty of treason, forgery, and shift,
Guilty of incest, that abomination
An accessary by thine inclination
    To all sins past, and all that are to come,
    From the creation to the general doom.

'Mis-shapen Time, copesmate of ugly Night,
Swift subtle post, carrier of grisly care,
Eater of youth, false slave to false delight,
Base watch of woes, sin's pack-horse, virtue's snare;
Thou nursest all, and murder'st all that are:
    O, hear me, then, injurious, shifting Time!
    Be guilty of my death, since of my crime.

'Why hath thy servant Opportunity
Betray'd the hours thou gavest me to repose,
Cancell'd my fortunes, and enchained me
To endless date of never-ending woes?
Time's office is to fine the hate of foes;
    To eat up errors by opinion bred,
    Not spend the dowry of a lawful bed.

'Time's glory is to calm contending kings,
To unmask falsehood, and bring truth to light,
To stamp the seal of time in aged things,
To wake the morn, and sentinel the night,
To wrong the wronger till he render right,
    To ruinate proud buildings with thy hours,
    And smear with dust their glittering golden towers;

'To fill with worm-holes stately monuments,
To feed oblivion with decay of things,
To blot old books and alter their contents,
To pluck the quills from ancient ravens' wings,
To dry the old oak's sap, and cherish springs,
    To spoil antiquities of hammer'd steel,
    And turn the giddy round of Fortune's wheel;

'To show the beldam daughters of her daughter,
To make the child a man, the man a child,
To slay the tiger that doth live by slaughter,
To tame the unicorn and lion wild,
To mock the subtle in themselves beguiled,
    To cheer the ploughman with increaseful crops,
    And waste huge stones with little water-drops.

'Why work'st thou mischief in thy pilgrimage,
Unless thou couldst return to make amends?
One poor retiring minute in an age
Would purchase thee a thousand thousand friends,
Lending him wit that to bad debtors lends:
    O, this dread night, wouldst thou one hour come back,
    I could prevent this storm, and shun thy wrack!

'Thou ceaseless lackey to eternity,
With some mischance cross Tarquin in his flight:
Devise extremes beyond extremity,
To make him curse this cursed crimeful night:
Let ghastly shadows his lewd eyes affright;
    And the dire thought of his committed evil
    Shape every bush a hideous shapeless devil.

'Disturb his hours of rest with restless trances,
Afflict him in his bed with bedrid groans;
Let there bechance him pitiful mischances,
To make him moan; but pity not his moans:
Stone him with harden'd hearts, harder than stones;
    And let mild women to him lose their mildness,
    Wilder to him than tigers in their wildness.

'Let him have time to tear his curled hair,
Let him have time against himself to rave,
Let him have time of Time's help to despair,
Let him have time to live a loathed slave,
Let him have time a beggar's orts to crave,
    And time to see one that by alms doth live
    Disdain to him disdained scraps to give.

'Let him have time to see his friends his foes,
And merry fools to mock at him resort;
Let him have time to mark how slow time goes
In time of sorrow, and how swift and short
His time of folly and his time of sport;
    And ever let his unrecalling crime
    Have time to wail th' abusing of his time.

'O Time, thou tutor both to good and bad,
Teach me to curse him that thou taught'st this ill!
At his own shadow let the thief run mad,
Himself himself seek every hour to kill!
Such wretched hands such wretched blood should spill;
    For who so base would such an office have
    As slanderous death's-man to so base a slave?

'The baser is he, coming from a king,
To shame his hope with deeds degenerate:
The mightier man, the mightier is the thing
That makes him honour'd, or begets him hate;
For greatest scandal waits on greatest state.
    The moon being clouded presently is mist,
    But little stars may hide them when they list.

'The crow may bathe his coal-black wings in mire,
And unperceived fly with the filth away;
But if the like the snow-white swan desire,
The stain upon his silver down will stay.
Poor grooms are sightless night, kings glorious day:
  Gnats are unnoted wheresoe'er they fly,
  But eagles gazed upon with every eye.

'Out, idle words, servants to shallow fools!
Unprofitable sounds, weak arbitrators!
Busy yourselves in skill-contending schools;
Debate where leisure serves with dull debaters;
To trembling clients be you mediators:
  For me, I force not argument a straw,
  Since that my case is past the help of law.

'In vain I rail at Opportunity,
At Time, at Tarquin, and uncheerful Night;
In vain I cavil with mine infamy,
In vain I spurn at my confirm'd despite:
This helpless smoke of words doth me no right.
  The remedy indeed to do me good
  Is to let forth my foul defiled blood.

'Poor hand, why quiver'st thou at this decree?
Honour thyself to rid me of this shame;
For if I die, my honour lives in thee;
But if I live, thou livest in my defame:
Since thou couldst not defend thy loyal dame,
  And wast afeard to scratch her wicked foe,
  Kill both thyself and her for yielding so.'

This said, from her betumbled couch she starteth,
To find some desperate instrument of death:
But this no slaughter-house no tool imparteth
To make more vent for passage of her breath;
Which, thronging through her lips, so vanisheth
  As smoke from Aetna, that in air consumes,
  Or that which from discharged cannon fumes.

'In vain,' quoth she, 'I live, and seek in vain
Some happy mean to end a hapless life.
I fear'd by Tarquin's falchion to be slain,
Yet for the self-same purpose seek a knife:
But when I fear'd I was a loyal wife:
  So am I now: – O no, that cannot be;
  Of that true type hath Tarquin rifled me.

'O, that is gone for which I sought to live,
And therefore now I need not fear to die.
To clear this spot by death, at least I give
A badge of fame to slander's livery;
A dying life to living infamy:
    Poor helpless help, the treasure stoln away,
    To burn the guiltless casket where it lay!

'Well, well, dear Collatine, thou shalt not know
The stained taste of violated troth;
I will not wrong thy true affection so,
To flatter thee with an infringed oath;
This bastard graff shall never come to growth:
    He shall not boast who did thy stock pollute
    That thou art doting father of his fruit.

'Nor shall he smile at thee in secret thought,
Nor laugh with his companions at thy state;
But thou shalt know thy interest was not bought
Basely with gold, but stoln from forth thy gate.
For me, I am the mistress of my fate,
    And with my trespass never will dispense,
    Till life to death acquit my forced offence.

'I will not poison thee with my attaint,
Nor fold my fault in cleanly-coin'd excuses;
My sable ground of sin I will not paint,
To hide the truth of this false night's abuses:
My tongue shall utter all; mine eyes, like sluices,
    As from a mountain-spring that feeds a dale,
    Shall gush pure streams to purge my impure tale.'

By this, lamenting Philomel had ended
The well-tuned warble of her nightly sorrow,
And solemn night with slow sad gait descended
To ugly hell; when, lo, the blushing morrow
Lends light to all fair eyes that light will borrow:
    But cloudy Lucrece shames herself to see,
    And therefore still in night would cloister'd be.

Revealing day through every cranny spies,
And seems to point her out where she sits weeping;
To whom she sobbing speaks: 'O eye of eyes,
Why pry'st thou through my window? leave thy peeping:
Mock with thy tickling beams eyes that are sleeping:
    Brand not my forehead with thy piercing light,
    For day hath naught to do what's done by night.'

Thus cavils she with every thing she sees:
True grief is fond and testy as a child,
Who wayward once, his mood with naught agrees:
Old woes, not infant sorrows, bear them mild;
Continuance tames the one; the other wild,
    Like an unpractised swimmer plunging still,
    With too much labour drowns for want of skill.

So she, deep-drenched in a sea of care,
Holds disputation with each thing she views,
And to herself all sorrow doth compare;
No object but her passion's strength renews;
And as one shifts, another straight ensues:
    Sometime her grief is dumb, and hath no words;
    Sometime 'tis mad, and too much talk affords.

The little birds that tune their morning's joy
Make her moans mad with their sweet melody:
For mirth doth search the bottom of annoy;
Sad souls are slain in merry company;
Grief best is pleased with grief's society:
    True sorrow then is feelingly suffic'd
    When with like semblance it is sympathized.

' 'Tis double death to drown in ken of shore;
He ten times pines that pines beholding food;
To see the salve doth make the wound ache more;
Great grief grieves most at that would do it good;
Deep woes roll forward like a gentle flood,
    Who, being stopt, the bounding banks o'erflows;
    Grief dallied with nor law nor limit knows.

'You mocking birds,' quoth she, 'your tunes entomb
Within your hollow swelling feather'd breasts,
And in my hearing be you mute and dumb:
My restless discord loves no stops nor rests;
A woeful hostess brooks not merry guests:
    Relish your nimble notes to pleasing ears;
    Distress likes dumps when time is kept with tears.

'Come, Philomel, that sing'st of ravishment,
Make thy sad grove in my dishevell'd hair:
As the dank earth weeps at thy languishment,
So I at each sad strain will strain a tear,
And with deep groans the diapason bear;
    For burthen-wise I'll hum on Tarquin still,
    While thou on Tereus descant'st better skill.

'And whiles against a thorn thou bear'st thy part,
To keep thy sharp woes waking. wretched I,
To imitate thee well, against my heart
Will fix a sharp knife, to affright mine eye;
Who, if it wink, shall thereon fall and die.
    These means, as frets upon an instrument,
    Shall tune our heart-strings to true languishment.

'And for, poor bird, thou sing'st not in the day,
As shaming any eye should thee behold,
Some dark-deep desert, seated from the way,
That knows not parching heat nor freezing cold,
Will we find out; and there we will unfold
    To creatures stern sad tunes, to change their kinds:
    Since men prove beasts, let beasts bear gentle minds.'

As the poor frighted deer, that stands at gaze,
Wildly determining which way to fly,
Or one encompast with a winding maze,
That cannot tread the way out readily;
So with herself is she in mutiny,
    To live or die, which of the twain were better,
    When life is shamed, and death reproach's debtor.

'To kill myself,' quoth she, 'alack, what were it,
But with my body my poor soul's pollution?
They that lose half with greater patience bear it
Than they whose whole is swallow'd in confusion.
That mother tries a merciless conclusion
    Who, having two sweet babes, when death takes one,
    Will slay the other, and be nurse to none.

'My body or my soul, which was the dearer,
When the one pure, the other made divine?
Whose love of either to myself was nearer,
When both were kept for heaven and Collatine?
Ay me! the bark pill'd from the lofty pine,
    His leaves will wither, and his sap decay;
    So must my soul, her bark being pill'd away.

'Her house is sackt, her quiet interrupted,
Her mansion batter'd by the enemy;
Her sacred temple spotted, spoil'd, corrupted,
Grossly engirt with daring infamy:
Then let it not be call'd impiety,
    If in this blemisht fort I make some hole
    Through which I may convey this troubled soul.

'Yet die I will not till my Collatine
Have heard the cause of my untimely death;
That he may vow, in that sad hour of mine,
Revenge on him that made me stop my breath.
My stained blood to Tarquin I'll bequeath,
    Which by him tainted shall for him be spent,
    And as his due writ in my testament.

'My honour I'll bequeath unto the knife
That wounds my body, so dishonoured.
'Tis honour to deprive dishonour'd life;
The one will live, the other being dead:
So of shame's ashes shall my fame be bred;
    For in my death I murder shameful scorn:
    My shame so dead, mine honour is new-born.

'Dear lord of that dear jewel I have lost,
What legacy shall I bequeath to thee?
My resolution, love, shall be thy boast,
By whose example thou revenged mayst be.
How Tarquin must be used, read it in me:
    Myself, thy friend, will kill myself, thy foe,
    And, for my sake, serve thou false Tarquin so.

'This brief abridgement of my will I make:
My soul and body to the skies and ground;
My resolution, husband, do thou take;
Mine honour be the knife's that makes my wound;
My shame be his that did my fame confound;
    And all my fame that lives disbursed be
    To those that live, and think no shame of me.

'Thou, Collatine, shalt oversee this will;
How was I overseen that thou shalt see it!
My blood shall wash the slander of mine ill;
My life's foul deed, my life's fair end shall free it.
Faint not, faint heart, but stoutly say "So be it:"
    Yield to my hand; my hand shall conquer thee:
    Thou dead, both die and both shall victors be.'

This plot of death when sadly she had laid,
And wiped the brinish pearl from her bright eyes,
With untuned tongue she hoarsely calls her maid,
Whose swift obedience to her mistress hies;
For fleet-wing'd duty with thought's feathers flies.
    Poor Lucrece' cheeks unto her maid seem so
    As winter meads when sun doth melt their snow.

Her mistress she doth give demure good-morrow,
With soft-slow tongue, true mark of modesty,
And sorts a sad look to her lady's sorrow,
For why her face wore sorrow's livery;
But durst not ask of her audaciously
 Why her two suns were cloud-eclipsed so,
 Nor why her fair cheeks overwasht with woe.

But as the earth doth weep, the sun being set,
Each flower moisten'd like a melting eye,
Even so the maid with swelling drops gan wet
Her circled eyne, enforced by sympathy
Of those fair suns set in her mistress' sky,
 Who in a salt-waved ocean quench their light,
 Which makes the maid weep like the dewy night.

A pretty while these pretty creatures stand,
Like ivory conduits coral cisterns filling:
One justly weeps; the other takes in hand
No cause, but company, of her drops spilling:
Their gentle sex to weep are often willing;
 Grieving themselves to guess at others' smarts,
 And then they drown their eyes, or break their hearts.

For men have marble, women waxen, minds,
And therefore are they form'd as marble will;
The weak opprest, the impression of strange kinds
Is form'd in them by force, by fraud, or skill:
Then call them not the authors of their ill,
 No more than wax shall be accounted evil
 Wherein is stampt the semblance of a devil.

Their smoothness, like a goodly champaign plain,
Lays open all the little worms that creep;
In men, as in a rough-grown grove, remain
Cave-keeping evils that obscurely sleep:
Through crystal walls each little mote will peep:
 Though men can cover crimes with bold stern looks,
 Poor women's faces are their own faults' books.

No man inveigh against the wither'd flower,
But chide rough winter that the flower hath kill'd:
Not that devour'd, but that which doth devour,
Is worthy blame. O, let it not be hild
Poor women's faults, that they are so fulfill'd
 With men's abuses: those proud lords, to blame,
 Make weak-made women tenants to their shame.

The precedent whereof in Lucrece view,
Assail'd by night with circumstances strong
Of present death, and shame that might ensue
By that her death, to do her husband wrong:
Such danger to resistance did belong,
    That dying fear through all her body spread;
    And who cannot abuse a body dead?

By this, mild patience bid fair Lucrece speak
To the poor counterfeit of her complaining:
'My girl,' quoth she, 'on what occasion break
Those tears from thee, that down thy cheeks are raining?
If thou dost weep for grief of my sustaining,
    Know, gentle wench, it small avails my mood:
    If tears could help, mine own would do me good.

'But tell me, girl, when went' - and there she stay'd
Till after a deep groan - 'Tarquin from hence?'
'Madam, ere I was up,' replied the maid,
'The more to blame my sluggard negligence:
Yet with the fault I thus far can dispense,
    Myself was stirring ere the break of day,
    And ere I rose was Tarquin gone away.

'But, lady, if your maid may be so bold
She would request to know your heaviness.'
'O, peace!' quoth Lucrece: 'if it should be told,
The repetition cannot make it less,
For more it is than I can well express:
    And that deep torture may be call'd a hell
    When more is felt than one hath power to tell.

'Go, get me hither paper, ink, and pen,
Yet save that labour, for I have them here.
What should I say? – One of my husband's men
Bid thou be ready, by and by, to bear
A letter to my lord, my love, my dear:
    Bid him with speed prepare to carry it;
    The cause craves haste, and it will soon be writ.'

Her maid is gone, and she prepares to write,
First hovering o'er the paper with her quill:
Conceit and grief an eager combat fight;
What wit sets down is blotted straight with will;
This is too curious-good, this blunt and ill:
    Much like a press of people at a door,
    Throng her inventions, which shall go before.

At last she thus begins: 'Thou worthy lord
Of that unworthy wife that greeteth thee,
Health to thy person! next vouchsafe t'afford —
If ever, love, thy Lucrece thou wilt see —
Some present speed to come and visit me.
    So, I commend me from our house in grief:
    My woes are tedious, though my words are brief.'

Here folds she up the tenour of her woe,
Her certain sorrow writ uncertainly.
By this short schedule Collatine may know
Her grief, but not her grief's true quality:
She dares not thereof make discovery,
    Lest he should hold it her own gross abuse,
    Ere she with blood had stain'd her stain'd excuse.

Besides, the life and feeling of her passion
She hoards, to spend when he is by to hear her;
When sighs and groans and tears may grace the fashion
Of her disgrace, the better so to clear her
From that suspicion which the world might bear her.
    To shun this blot, she would not blot the letter
    With words, till action might become them better.

To see sad sights moves more than hear them told;
For then the eye interprets to the ear
The heavy motion that it doth behold,
When every part a part of woe doth bear.
'Tis but a part of sorrow that we hear:
    Deep sounds make lesser noise than shallow fords,
    And sorrow ebbs, being blown with wind of words.

Her letter now is seal'd, and on it writ,
'At Ardea to my lord with more than haste.'
The post attends, and she delivers it,
Charging the sour-faced groom to hie as fast
As lagging fowls before the northern blast:
    Speed more than speed but dull and slow she deems:
    Extremity still urgeth such extremes.

The homely villain court'sies to her low;
And, blushing on her, with a steadfast eye
Receives the scroll without or yea or no,
And forth with bashful innocence doth hie.
But they whose guilt within their bosoms lie
    Imagine every eye beholds their blame;
    For Lucrece thought he blusht to see her shame:

When, silly groom! God wot, it was defect
Of spirit, life, and bold audacity.
Such harmless creatures have a true respect
To talk in deeds, while others saucily
Promise more speed, but do it leisurely:
 Even so this pattern of the worn-out age
 Pawn'd honest looks, but laid no words to gage.

His kindled duty kindled her mistrust,
That two red fires in both their faces blazed;
She thought he blusht, as knowing Tarquin's lust,
And, blushing with him, wistly on him gazed;
Her earnest eye did make him more amazed:
 The more she saw the blood his cheeks replenish,
 The more she thought he spied in her some blemish.

But long she thinks till he return again,
And yet the duteous vassal scarce is gone.
The weary time she cannot entertain,
For now 'tis stale to sigh, to weep, and groan:
So woe hath wearied woe, moan tired moan,
 That she her plaints a little while doth stay,
 Pausing for means to mourn some newer way.

At last she calls to mind where hangs a piece
Of skilful painting, made for Priam's Troy;
Before the which is drawn the power of Greece,
For Helen's rape the city to destroy,
Threatening cloud-kissing lion with annoy;
 Which the conceited painter drew so proud,
 As heaven, it seem'd, to kiss the turrets bow'd.

A thousand lamentable objects there,
In scorn of nature, art gave lifeless life:
Many a dry drop seem'd a weeping tear,
Shed for the slaughter'd husband by the wife:
The red blood reekt, to show the painter's strife;
 And dying eyes gleam'd forth their ashy lights,
 Like dying coals burnt out in tedious nights.

There might you see the labouring pioner
Begrimed with sweat, and smeared all with dust;
And from the towers of Troy there would appear
The very eyes of men through loop-holes thrust,
Gazing upon the Greeks with little lust:
 Such sweet observance in this work was had,
 That one might see those far-off eyes look sad.

In great commanders grace and majesty
You might behold, triumphing in their faces;
In youth, quick bearing and dexterity;
And here and there the painter interlaces
Pale cowards, marching on with trembling paces;
    Which heartless peasants did so well resemble
    That one would swear he saw them quake and tremble.

In Ajax and Ulysses, O, what art
Of physiognomy might one behold!
The face of either cipher'd either's heart;
Their face their manners most expressly told:
In Ajax' eyes blunt rage and rigour roll'd;
    But the mild glance that sly Ulysses lent
    Show'd deep regard and smiling government.

There pleading might you see grave Nestor stand,
As 'twere encouraging the Greeks to fight:
Making such sober action with his hand,
That it beguiled attention, charm'd the sight:
In speech, it seem'd, his beard, all silver white,
    Wagg'd up and down, and from his lips did fly
    Thin winding breath, which purl'd up to the sky.

About him were a press of gaping faces,
Which seem'd to swallow up his sound advice;
All jointly listening, but with several graces,
As if some mermaid did their ears entice,
Some high, some low, – the painter was so nice;
    The scalps of many, almost hid behind,
    To jump up higher seem'd, to mock the mind.

Here one man's hand lean'd on another's head,
His nose being shadow'd by his neighbour's ear;
Here one, being throng'd, bears back, all boln and red;
Another, smother'd, seems to pelt and swear;
And in their rage such signs of rage they bear,
    As, but for loss of Nestor's golden words,
    It seem'd they would debate with angry swords.

For much imaginary work was there;
Conceit deceitful, so compact, so kind,
That for Achilles' image stood his spear,
Griped in an armed hand, himself, behind,
Was left unseen, save to the eye of mind:
    A hand, a foot, a face, a leg, a head,
    Stood for the whole to be imagined.

And from the walls of strong-besieged Troy
When their brave hope, bold Hector, marcht to field
Stood many Trojan mothers, sharing joy
To see their youthful sons bright weapons wield;
And to their hope they such odd action yield,
 That through their light joy seemed to appear,
 Like bright things stain'd, a kind of heavy fear.

And from the strond of Dardan, where they fought,
To Simois' reedy banks the red blood ran,
Whose waves to imitate the battle sought
With swelling ridges; and their ranks began
To break upon the galled shore, and than
 Retire again, till meeting greater ranks,
 They join, and shoot their foam at Simois' banks.

To this well-painted piece is Lucrece come,
To find a face where all distress is stell'd.
Many she sees where cares have carved some,
But none where all distress and dolour dwell'd,
Till she despairing Hecuba beheld,
 Staring on Priam's wounds with her old eyes,
 Which bleeding under Pyrrhus' proud foot lies.

In her the painter had anatomized
Time's ruin, beauty's wrack, and grim care's reign:
Her cheeks with chops and wrinkles were disguised;
Of what she was no semblance did remain:
Her blue blood changed to black in every vein,
 Wanting the spring that those shrunk pipes had fed,
 Show'd life imprison'd in a body dead.

On this sad shadow Lucrece spends her eyes,
And shapes her sorrow to the beldam's woes,
Who nothing wants to answer her but cries,
And bitter words to ban her cruel foes:
The painter was no god to lend her those;
 And therefore Lucrece swears he did her wrong,
 To give her so much grief, and not a tongue.

'Poor instrument,' quoth she, 'without a sound,
I'll tune thy woes with my lamenting tongue;
And drop sweet balm in Priam's painted wound,
And rail on Pyrrhus that hath done him wrong;
And with my tears quench Troy that burns so long;
 And with my knife scratch out the angry eyes
 Of all the Greeks that are thine enemies.

Show me the strumpet that began this stir,
That with my nails her beauty I may tear.
Thy heat of lust, fond Paris, did incur
This load of wrath that burning Troy doth bear:
Thy eye kindled the fire that burneth here;
    And here in Troy, for trespass of thine eye,
    The sire, the son, the dame, and daughter die.

'Why should the private pleasure of some one
Become the public plague of many moe?
Let sin, alone committed, light alone
Upon his head that hath transgressed so;
Let guiltless souls be freed from guilty woe:
    For one's offence why should so many fall,
    To plague a private sin in general?

'Lo, here weeps Hecuba, here Priam dies,
Here manly Hector faints, here Troilus swounds,
Here friend by friend in bloody channel lies,
And friend to friend gives unadvised wounds,
And one man's lust these many lives confounds:
    Had doting Priam checkt his son's desire,
    Troy had been bright with fame, and not with fire.'

Here feelingly she weeps Troy's painted woes:
For sorrow, like a heavy-hanging bell,
Once set on ringing, with his own weight goes;
Then little strength rings out the doleful knell:
So Lucrece, set a-work, sad tales doth tell
    To pencill'd pensiveness and colour'd sorrow;
    She lends them words, and she their looks doth borrow.

She throws her eyes about the painting round,
And who she finds forlorn she doth lament.
At last she sees a wretched image bound,
That piteous looks to Phrygian shepherds lent:
His face, though full of cares, yet show'd content;
    Onward to Troy with the blunt swains he goes,
    So mild that Patience seem'd to scorn his woes.

In him the painter labour'd with his skill
To hide deceit, and give the harmless show
An humble gait, calm looks, eyes wailing still,
A brow unbent, that seem'd to welcome woe;
Cheeks neither red nor pale, but mingled so
    That blushing red no guilty instance gave,
    Nor ashy pale the fear that false hearts have.

But, like a constant and confirmed devil,
He entertain'd a show so seeming just,
And therein so ensconced his secret evil,
That jealousy itself could not mistrust
False-creeping craft and perjury should thrust
    Into so bright a day such black-faced storms,
    Or blot with hell-born sin such saint-like forms.

The well-skill'd workman this mild image drew
For perjured Sinon, whose enchanting story
The credulous old Priam after slew;
Whose words, like wildfire, burnt the shining glory
Of rich-built Ilion, that the skies were sorry,
    And little stars shot from their fixed places,
    When their glass fell wherein they view'd their faces.

This picture she advisedly perused,
And chid the painter for his wondrous skill,
Saying, some shape in Sinon's was abused;
So fair a form lodged not a mind so ill:
And still on him she gazed, and gazing still,
    Such signs of truth in his plain face she spied,
    That she concludes the picture was belied.

'It cannot be,' quoth she, 'that so much guile' –
She would have said 'can lurk in such a look;'
But Tarquin's shape came in her mind the while,
And from her tongue 'can lurk' from 'cannot' took:
'It cannot be' she in that sense forsook,
    And turn'd it thus, 'It cannot be, I find,
    But such a face should bear a wicked mind:

'For even as subtle Sinon here is painted,
So sober-sad, so weary, and so mild,
As if with grief or travail he had fainted,
To me came Tarquin armed; so beguiled
With outward honesty, but yet defiled
    With inward vice: as Priam him did cherish,
    So did I Tarquin; so my Troy did perish.

'Look, look, how listening Priam wets his eyes,
To see those borrow'd tears that Sinon sheeds!
Priam, why art thou old, and yet not wise?
For every tear he falls a Trojan bleeds:
His eye drops fire, no water thence proceeds;
    Those round clear pearls of his, that move thy pity,
    Are balls of quenchless fire to burn thy city.

'Such devils steal effects from lightless hell;
For Sinon in his fire doth quake with cold,
And in that cold hot-burning fire doth dwell;
These contraries such unity do hold,
Only to flatter fools, and make them bold:
    So Priam's trust false Sinon's tears doth flatter,
    That he finds means to burn his Troy with water.'

Here, all enraged, such passion her assails,
That patience is quite beaten from her breast.
She tears the senseless Sinon with her nails,
Comparing him to that unhappy guest
Whose deed hath made herself herself detest:
    At last she smilingly with this gives o'er;
    'Fool, fool!' quoth she, 'his wounds will not be sore.'

Thus ebbs and flows the current of her sorrow,
And time doth weary time with her complaining.
She looks for night, and then she longs for morrow,
And both she thinks too long with her remaining;
Short time seems long in sorrow's sharp sustaining:
    Though woe be heavy, yet it seldom sleeps;
    And they that watch see time how slow it creeps.

Which all this time hath overslipt her thought.
That she with painted images hath spent;
Being from the feeling of her own grief brought
By deep surmise of others' detriment;
Losing her woes in shows of discontent.
    It easeth some, though none it ever cured,
    To think their dolour others have endured.

But now the mindful messenger, come back,
Brings home his lord and other company:
Who finds his Lucrece clad in mourning black;
And round about her tear-distained eye
Blue circles stream'd, like rainbows in the sky:
    These water-galls in her dim element
    Foretell new storms to those already spent.

Which when her sad-beholding husband saw,
Amazedly in her sad face he stares:
Her eyes, though sod in tears, lookt red and raw,
Her lively colour kill'd with deadly cares.
He hath no power to ask her how she fares;
    Both stood, like old acquaintance in a trance,
    Met far from home, wondering each other's chance.

At last he takes her by the bloodless hand,
And thus begins: 'What uncouth ill event
Hath thee befaln, that thou dost trembling stand?
Sweet love, what spite hath thy fair colour spent?
Why art thou thus attired in discontent?
    Unmask, dear dear, this moody heaviness,
    And tell thy grief, that we may give redress.'

Three times with sighs she gives her sorrow fire,
Ere once she can discharge one word of woe:
At length addrest to answer his desire,
She modestly prepares to let them know
Her honour is ta'en prisoner by the foe;
    While Collatine and his consorted lords
    With sad attention long to hear her words.

And now this pale swan in her watery nest
Begins the sad dirge of her certain ending:
'Few words,' quoth she, 'shall fit the trespass best,
Where no excuse can give the fault amending:
In me moe woes than words are now depending;
    And my laments would be drawn out too long,
    To tell them all with one poor tired tongue.

'Then be this all the task it hath to say:
Dear husband, in the interest of thy bed
A stranger came, and on that pillow lay
Where thou wast wont to rest thy weary head;
And what wrong else may be imagined
    By foul enforcement might be done to me,
    From that, alas, thy Lucrece is not free.

'For in the dreadful dead of dark midnight,
With shining falchion in my chamber came
A creeping creature, with a flaming light,
And softly cried, "Awake, thou Roman dame.
And entertain my love; else lasting shame
    On thee and thine this night I will inflict,
    If thou my love's desire do contradict.

' "For some hard-favour'd groom of thine," quoth he,
"Unless thou yoke thy liking to my will,
I'll murder straight, and then I'll slaughter thee,
And swear I found you where you did fulfil
The loathsome act of lust, and so did kill
    The lechers in their deed: this act will be
    My fame, and thy perpetual infamy."

'With this, I did begin to start and cry;
And then against my heart he set his sword,
Swearing, unless I took all patiently,
I should not live to speak another word;
So should my shame still rest upon record,
    And never be forgot in mighty Rome
    Th' adulterate death of Lucrece and her groom.

'Mine enemy was strong, my poor self weak,
And far the weaker with so strong a fear:
My bloody judge forbade my tongue to speak;
No rightful plea might plead for justice there:
His scarlet lust came evidence to swear
    That my poor beauty had purloin'd his eyes;
    And when the judge is robb'd, the prisoner dies.

'O, teach me how to make mine own excuse!
Or, at the least, this refuge let me find,
Though my gross blood be stain'd with this abuse,
Immaculate and spotless is my mind;
That was not forced; that never was inclined
    To accessary yieldings, but still pure
    Doth in her poison'd closet yet endure.'

Lo, here, the hopeless merchant of this loss,
With head declined, and voice damm'd up with woe,
With sad-set eyes, and wretched arms across,
From lips new-waxen pale begins to blow
The grief away that stops his answer so:
    But, wretched as he is, he strives in vain;
    What he breathes out his breath drinks up again.

As through an arch the violent roaring tide
Outruns the eye that doth behold his haste,
Yet in the eddy boundeth in his pride
Back to the strait that forced him on so fast;
In rage sent out, recall'd in rage, being past:
    Even so his sighs, his sorrows, make a saw,
    To push grief on, and back the same grief draw.

Which speechless woe of his poor she attendeth,
And his untimely frenzy thus awaketh:
'Dear lord, thy sorrow to my sorrow lendeth
Another power; no flood by raining slaketh.
My woe too sensible thy passion maketh
    More feeling-painful: let it, then, suffice
    To drown one woe, one pair of weeping eyes.

'And for my sake, when I might charm thee so,
For she that was thy Lucrece, – now attend me:
Be suddenly revenged on my foe,
Thine, mine, his own: suppose thou dost defend me
From what is past: the help that thou shalt lend me
    Comes all too late, yet let the traitor die;
    For sparing justice feeds iniquity.

'But ere I name him, you fair lords', quoth she,
Speaking to those that came with Collatine,
'Shall plight your honourable faiths to me,
With swift pursuit to venge this wrong of mine;
For 'tis a meritorious fair design
    To chase injustice with revengeful arms:
    Knights, by their oaths, should right poor ladies' harms.'

At this request, with noble disposition
Each present lord began to promise aid,
As bound in knighthood to her imposition,
Longing to hear the hateful foe bewray'd.
But she, that yet her sad task hath not said,
    The protestation stops. 'O, speak,' quoth she,
    'How may this forced stain be wiped from me?

'What is the quality of mine offence,
Being constrain'd with dreadful circumstance?
May my pure mind with the foul act dispense,
My low-declined honour to advance?
May any terms acquit me from this chance?
    The poison'd fountain clears itself again;
    And why not I from this compelled stain?'

With this, they all at once began to say,
Her body's stain her mind untainted clears;
While with a joyless smile she turns away
The face, that map which deep impression bears
Of hard misfortune, carved in it with tears.
    'No, no,' quoth she, 'no dame, hereafter living,
    By my excuse shall claim excuse's giving.'

Here with a sigh, as if her heart would break,
She throws forth Tarquin's name: 'He, he,' she says,
But more than 'he' her poor tongue could not speak;
Till after many accents and delays,
Untimely breathings, sick and short assays,
    She utters this, 'He, he, fair lords, 'tis he
    That guides this hand to give this wound to me.'

Even here she sheathed in her harmless breast
A harmful knife, that thence her soul unsheathed:
That blow did bail it from the deep unrest
Of that polluted prison where it breathed:
Her contrite sighs unto the clouds bequeathed
    Her winged sprite, and through her wounds doth fly
    Life's lasting date from cancell'd destiny.

Stone-still, astonisht with this deadly deed,
Stood Collatine and all his lordly crew;
Till Lucrece' father, that beholds her bleed,
Himself on her self-slaughter'd body threw;
And from the purple fountain Brutus drew
    The murderous knife, and, as it left the place,
    Her blood, in poor revenge, held it in chase;

And bubbling from her breast, it doth divide
In two slow rivers, that the crimson blood
Circles her body in on every side,
Who, like a late-sackt island, vastly stood
Bare and unpeopled in this fearful flood.
    Some of her blood still pure and red remain'd,
    And some lookt black, and that false Tarquin stain'd.

About the mourning and congealed face
Of that black blood a watery rigol goes,
Which seems to weep upon the tainted place:
And ever since, as pitying Lucrece' woes,
Corrupted blood some watery token shows;
    And blood untainted still doth red abide,
    Blushing at that which is so putrefied.

'Daughter, dear daughter,' old Lucretius cries,
'That life was mine which thou hast here deprived.
If in the child the father's image lies,
Where shall I live now Lucrece is unlived?
Thou wast not to this end from me derived.
    If children pre-decease progenitors,
    We are their offspring, and they none of ours.

'Poor broken glass, I often did behold
In thy sweet semblance my old age new born;
But now that fair fresh mirror, dim and old,
Shows me a bare-boned death by time outworn:
O, from thy cheeks my image thou hast torn,
    And shiver'd all the beauty of my glass,
    That I no more can see what once I was.

'O time, cease thou thy course, and last no longer,
If they surcease to be that should survive.
Shall rotten death make conquest of the stronger,
And leave the faltering feeble souls alive?
The old bees die, the young possess their hive:
    Then live, sweet Lucrece, live again, and see
    Thy father die, and not thy father thee.'

By this, starts Collatine as from a dream,
And bids Lucretius give his sorrow place;
And then in key-cold Lucrece' bleeding stream
He falls, and bathes the pale fear in his face,
And counterfeits to die with her a space;
    Till manly shame bids him possess his breath,
    And live to be revenged on her death.

The deep vexation of his inward soul
Hath served a dumb arrest upon his tongue;
Who, mad that sorrow should his use control,
Or keep him from heart-easing words so long,
Begins to talk; but through his lips do throng
    Weak words, so thick come in his poor heart's aid,
    That no man could distinguish what he said.

Yet sometime 'Tarquin' was pronounced plain,
But through his teeth, as if the name he tore.
This windy tempest, till it blow up rain,
Held back his sorrow's tide. to make it more;
At last it rains, and busy winds give o'er:
    The son and father weep with equal strife
    Who should weep most, for daughter or for wife.

The one doth call her his, the other his,
Yet neither may possess the claim they lay.
The father says 'She's mine.' 'O, mine she is,'
Replies her husband: 'do not take away
My sorrow's interest; let no mourner say
    He weeps for her, for she was only mine,
    And only must be wail'd by Collatine.'

'O,' quoth Lucretius, 'I did give that life
Which she too early and too late hath spill'd.'
'Woe, woe,' quoth Collatine, 'she was my wife,
I owed her, and 'tis mine that she hath kill'd.'
'My daughter' and 'my wife' with clamours fill'd
    The dispersed air, who, holding Lucrece' life,
    Answer'd their cries, 'my daughter' and 'my wife.'

Brutus, who pluckt the knife from Lucrece' side,
Seeing such emulation in their woe,
Began to clothe his wit in state and pride,
Burying in Lucrece' wound his folly's show.
He with the Romans was esteemed so
    As silly-jeering idiots are with kings,
    For sportive words and uttering foolish things:

But now he throws that shallow habit by,
Wherein deep policy did him disguise;
And arm'd his long-hid wits advisedly,
To check the tears in Collatinus' eyes.
'Thou wronged lord of Rome,' quoth he, 'arise:
    Let my unsounded self, supposed a fool,
    Now set thy long-experienced wit to school.

'Why, Collatine, is woe the cure for woe?
Do wounds help wounds, or grief help grievous deeds?
Is it revenge to give thyself a blow
For his foul act by whom thy fair wife bleeds?
Such childish humour from weak minds proceeds:
    Thy wretched wife mistook the matter so,
    To slay herself, that should have slain her foe.

'Courageous Roman, do not steep thy heart
In such relenting dew of lamentations;
But kneel with me, and help to bear thy part,
To rouse our Roman gods with invocations,
That they will suffer these abominations,
    Since Rome herself in them doth stand disgraced,
    By our strong arms from forth her fair streets chased.

'Now, by the Capitol that we adore,
And by this chaste blood so unjustly stained,
By heaven's fair sun that breeds the fat earth's store,
By all our country rights in Rome maintained,
And by chaste Lucrece' soul that late complained
    Her wrongs to us, and by this bloody knife,
    We will revenge the death of this true wife.'

This said, he struck his hand upon his breast,
And kist the fatal knife, to end his vow;
And to his protestation urged the rest,
Who, wondering at him, did his words allow:
Then jointly to the ground their knees they bow;
    And that deep vow, which Brutus made before,
    He doth again repeat, and that they swore.

Then they had sworn to this advised doom,
They did conclude to bear dead Lucrece thence.
To show her bleeding body thorough Rome,
And so to publish Tarquin's foul offence:
Which being done with speedy diligence,
    The Romans plausibly did give consent
    To Tarquin's everlasting banishment.

WHAT A DRAMA!

One of the meanings of the word is expressed in The Oxford Reference Dictionary as: 'a dramatic series of events; dramatic quality'.

Life is full of drama. Without it there would be no great plays, no mesmerising television series, no Hollywood scriptwriters, no plays in the London Theatre, no Agatha Christie, no Sherlock Holmes.

It's pointless going on.

Shakespeare was a dramatist, and therefore even in his poetry (apart from his sonnets and love poems) he had to present his theme in dramatic form. So when Sir Philip Sidney (1554-1586), William Hazlitt (1778-1830) and Samuel Taylor Coleridge (1772-1834) referred to *The Rape of Lucrece* as 'a lack of feeling', an 'ice-house' or 'lacking in pathos', perhaps they missed the point.

Shakespeare's *'Rape of Lucretia'* is believed to be a grim tragedy from Roman history. It is also a grim tragedy from all human life.

Shakespeare was a great poet, and great poets need poet's licence. So this version is full of ornamented language and a self-conscious delight in verbal artifice.

Sidney, Hazlitt and Coleridge were not dramatists, although Coleridge had a great deal of dramatic presentation in his *'Rime of the Ancient Mariner'* (1798).

In the heart of London with plagues, murder and lots of ale (the water must have been unsafe) Shakespeare knew his audience.

The wonder is that he was able to write such lengthy poems with such a remarkable choice of words and rhymes, and with such a consistency of his chosen rhyme pattern.

He established himself with *Venus and Adonis* and the *Rape of Lucrece*. He could not have realised that his great dramatic plays would be performed far more effectively on stage, screen and television.

A LOVER'S COMPLAINT

From off a hill whose concave womb re-worded
A plaintful story from a sistering vale,
My spirits t'attend this double voice accorded,
And down I laid to list the sad-tuned tale;
Ere long espied a fickle maid full pale,
Tearing of papers, breaking rings a-twain,
Storming her world with sorrow's wind and rain.

Upon her head a platted hive of straw,
Which fortified her visage from the sun,
Whereon the thought might think sometime it saw
The carcass of a beauty spent and done:
Time had not scythed all that youth begun,
Nor youth all quit; but, spite of heaven's fell rage,
Some beauty peept through lattice of sear'd age.

Oft did she heave her napkin to her eyne,
Which on it had conceited characters,
Laundering the silken figures in the brine
That season'd woe had pelleted in tears,
And often reading what contents it bears;
As often shrieking undistinguisht woe,
In clamours of all size, both high and low.

Sometimes her levell'd eyes their carriage ride,
As they did battery to the spheres intend;
Sometime diverted their poor balls are tied
To th' orbed earth; sometimes they do extend
Their view right on; anon their gazes lend
To every place at once, and, nowhere fixt,
The mind and sight distractedly commixt.

Her hair, nor loose nor tied in formal plat,
Proclaim'd in her a careless hand of pride;
For some, untuckt, descended her sheaved hat,
Hanging her pale and pined cheek beside;
Some in her threaden fillet still did bide,
And, true to bondage, would not break from thence,
Though slackly braided in loose negligence.

A thousand favours from a maund she drew
Of amber, crystal, and of beaded jet,
Which one by one she in a river threw,
Upon whose weeping margent she was set;
Like usury, applying wet to wet,
Or monarch's hands that lets not bounty fall
Where want cries some, but where excess begs all.

Of folded schedules had she many a one,
Which she perused, sigh'd, tore, and gave the flood;
Crackt many a ring of posied gold and bone,
Bidding them find their sepulchres in mud;
Found yet moe letters sadly penn'd in blood,
With sleided silk feat and affectedly
Enswathed, and seal'd to curious secrecy.

These often bathed she in her fluxive eyes,
And often kist, and often gan to tear;
Cried, 'O false blood, thou register of lies,
What unapproved witness dost thou bear!
Ink would have seem'd more black and damned here!'
This said, in top of rage the lines she rents,
Big discontent so breaking their contents.

A reverend man that grazed his cattle nigh –
Sometime a blusterer, that the ruffle knew
Of court, of city, and had let go by
The swiftest hours, observed as they flew
Towards this afflicted fancy fastly drew,
And, privileged by age, desires to know
In brief the grounds and motives of her woe.

So slides he down upon his grained bat,
And comely-distant sits he by her side;
When he again desires her, being sat,
Her grievance with his hearing to divide:
If that from him there may be aught applied
Which may her suffering ecstasy assuage,
'Tis promised in the charity of age.

'Father,' she says, 'though in me you behold
The injury of many a blasting hour,
Let it not tell your judgement I am old;
Not age, but sorrow, over me hath power:
I might as yet have been a spreading flower,
Fresh to myself, if I had self-applied
Love to myself, and to no love beside.

'But, woe is me! too early I attended
A youthful suit – it was to gain my grace –
Of one by nature's outwards so commended,
That maidens' eyes stuck over all his face:
Love lackt a dwelling, and made him her place;
And when in his fair parts she did abide,
She was new lodged, and newly deified.

'His browny locks did hang in crooked curls;
And every light occasion of the wind
Upon his lips their silken parcels hurls.
What's sweet to do, to do will aptly find:
Each eye that saw him did enchant the mind;
For on his visage was in little drawn
What largeness thinks in Paradise was sawn.

'Small show of man was yet upon his chin;
His phoenix down began but to appear,
Like unshorn velvet, on that termless skin,
Whose bare out-bragg'd the web it seem'd to wear:
Yet show'd his visage by that cost more dear;
And nice affections wavering stood in doubt
If best were as it was, or best without.

'His qualities were beauteous as his form,
For maiden-tongued he was, and thereof free;
Yet, if men moved him, was he such a storm
As oft 'twixt May and April is to see,
When winds breathe sweet, unruly though they be.
His rudeness so with his authorized youth
Did livery falseness in a pride of truth.

'Well could he ride, and often men would say,
"That horse his mettle from his rider takes:
Proud of subjection, noble by the sway,
What rounds, what bounds, what course, what stop he makes!"
And controversy hence a question takes,
Whether the horse by him became his deed,
Or he his manage by the well-doing steed.

'But quickly on this side the verdict went:
His real habitude gave life and grace
To appertainings and to ornament,
Accomplisht in himself, not in his case:
All aids, themselves made fairer by their place,
Came for additions; yet their purposed trim
Pieced not his grace, but were all graced by him.

'So on the tip of his subduing tongue
All kind of arguments and question deep,
All replication prompt, and reason strong,
For his advantage still did wake and sleep:
To make the weeper laugh, the laugher weep,
He had the dialect and different skill,
Catching all passions in his craft of will:

'That he did in the general bosom reign
Of young, of old; and sexes both enchanted,
To dwell with him in thoughts, or to remain
In personal duty, following where he haunted:
Consents bewitcht, ere he desire, have granted;
And dialogued for him what he would say,
Askt their own wills, and made their wills obey.

'Many there were that did his picture get,
To serve their eyes, and in it put their mind;
Like fools that in th' imagination set
The goodly objects which abroad they find
Of lands and mansions, theirs in thought assign'd;
And labouring in moe pleasures to bestow them
Than the true gouty landlord which doth owe them:

'So many have, that never toucht his hand,
Sweetly supposed them mistress of his heart.
My woeful self, that did in freedom stand,
And was my own fee-simple, not in part,
What with his art in youth, and youth in art,
Threw my affections in his charmed power,
Reserved the stalk, and gave him all my flower.

'Yet did I not, as some my equals did,
Demand of him, nor being desired yielded;
Finding myself in honour so forbid,
With safest distance I mine honour shielded:
Experience for me many bulwarks builded
Of proofs new-bleeding, which remain'd the foil
Of this false jewel, and his amorous spoil.

'But, ah, who ever shunn'd by precedent
The destined ill she must herself assay?
Or forced examples, 'gainst her own content,
To put the by-past perils in her way?
Counsel may stop awhile what will not stay;
For when we rage, advice is often seen
By blunting us to make our wits more keen.

'Nor gives it satisfaction to our blood,
That we must curb it upon others' proof;
To be forbod the sweets that seem so good,
For fear of harms that preach in our behoof.
O appetite, from judgement stand aloof.
The one a palate hath that needs will taste,
Though Reason weep, and cry, "it is thy last."

'For further I could say, "This man's untrue,"
And knew the patterns of his foul beguiling;
Heard where his plants in others' orchards grew,
Saw how deceits were gilded in his smiling;
Knew vows were ever brokers to defiling;
Thought characters and words merely but art,
And bastards of his foul adulterate heart.

'And long upon these terms I held my city,
Till thus he gan besiege me: "Gentle maid,
Have of my suffering youth some feeling pity,
And be not of my holy vows afraid:
That's to ye sworn to none was ever said;
For feasts of love I have been call'd unto,
Till now did ne'er invite, nor never woo.

' "All my offences that abroad you see
Are errors of the blood, none of the mind;
Love made them not; with acture they may be,
Where neither party is nor true nor kind:
They sought their shame that so their shame did find;
And so much less of shame in me remains,
But how much of me their reproach contains.

' "Among the many that mine eyes have seen,
Not one whose flame my heart so much as warmed,
Or my affection put to the smallest teen,
Or any of my leisures ever charmed:
Harm have I done to them, but ne'er was harmed;
Kept hearts in liveries, but mine own was free,
And reign'd, commanding in his monarchy.

' "Look here, what tributes wounded fancies sent me,
Of paled pearls and rubies red as blood;
Figuring that they their passions likewise lent me
Of grief and blushes, aptly understood
In bloodless white and the encrimson'd mood;
Effects of terror and dear modesty,
Encampt in hearts, but fighting outwardly.

' "And, lo, behold these talents of their hair,
With twisted metal amorously impleacht,
I have received from many a several fair –,
Their kind acceptance weepingly beseecht, –
With the annexions of fair gems enricht,
And deep-brain'd sonnets that did amplify
Each stone's dear nature, worth, and quality.

' "The diamond, – why, 'twas beautiful and hard,
Whereto his invised properties did tend;
The deep-green emerald, in whose fresh regard
Weak sights their sickly radiance do amend;
The heaven-hued sapphire, and the opal blend
With objects manifold: each several stone,
With wit well blazon'd, smiled or made some moan.

' "Lo, all these trophies of affections hot,
Of pensived and subdued desires the tender,
Nature hath charged me that I hoard them not,
But yield them up where I myself must render,
That is, to you, my origin and ender;
For these, of force, must your oblations be,
Since I their altar, you enpatron me.

' "O, then, advance of yours that phraseless hand,
Whose white weighs down the airy scale of praise;
Take all these similes to your own command,
Hallow'd with sighs that burning lungs did raise;
What me your minister, for you obeys,
Works under you; and to your audit comes
Their distract parcels in combined sums.

' "Lo, this device was sent me from a nun,
A sister sanctified, of holiest note;
Which late her noble suit in court did shun,
Whose rarest havings made the blossoms dote;
For she was sought by spirits of richest coat,
But kept cold distance, and did thence remove,
To spend her living in eternal love.

' "But, O my sweet, what labour is't to leave
The thing we have not, mastering what not strives, –
Paling the place which did no form receive,
Playing patient sports in unconstrained gyves?
She that her fame so to herself contrives,
The scars of battle scapeth by the flight,
And makes her absence valiant, not her might.

' "O, pardon me, in that my boast is true:
The accident which brought me to her eye
Upon the moment did her force subdue,
And now she would the caged cloister fly:
Religious love put out Religion's eye:
Not to be tempted, would she be immured,
And now, to tempt all, liberty procured.

' "How mighty, then, you are, O, hear me tell!
The broken bosoms that to me belong
Have emptied all their fountains in my well,
And mine I pour your ocean all among:
I strong o'er them, and you o'er me being strong,
Must for your victory us all congest,
As compound love to physic your cold breast.

' "My parts had power to charm a sacred nun,
Who, disciplined, ay, dieted in grace,
Believed her eyes when they t'assail begun,
All vows and consecrations giving place:
O most potential love! vow, bond, nor space,
In thee hath neither sting, knot, nor confine,
For thou art all, and all things else are thine.

' "When thou impressest, what are precepts worth
Of stale example? When thou wilt inflame,
How coldly those impediments stand forth
Of wealth, of filial fear, law, kindred, fame!
Love's arms are peace, 'gainst rule, 'gainst sense, 'gainst shame:
And sweetens, in the suffering pangs it bears,
The aloes of all forces, shocks, and fears.

' "Now all these hearts that do on mine depend,
Feeling it break, with bleeding groans they pine;
And supplicant their sighs to you extend,
To leave the battery that you make 'gainst mine,
Lending soft audience to my sweet design;
And credent soul to that strong-bonded oath
That shall prefer and undertake my troth."

'This said, his watery eyes he did dismount,
Whose sights till then were levell'd on my face;
Each cheek a river running from a fount
With brinish current downward flow'd apace:
O, how the channel to the stream gave grace!
Who glazed with crystal gate the glowing roses
That name through water which their hue encloses.

'O father, what a hell of witchcraft lies
In the small orb of one particular tear!
But with the inundation of the eyes
What rocky heart to water will not wear?
What breast so cold that is not warmed here?
O cleft effect! cold modesty, hot wrath,
Both fire from hence and chill extincture hath.

'For, lo, his passion, but an art of craft,
Even there resolved my reason into tears;
There my white stole of chastity I daft,
Shook off my sober guards and civil fears;
Appear to him, as he to me appears,
All melting; though our drops this difference bore,
His poison'd me, and mine did him restore.

'In him a plenitude of subtle matter,
Applied to cautels, all strange forms receives,
Of burning blushes, or of weeping water,
Or swounding paleness; and he takes and leaves,
In either's aptness, as it best deceives,
To blush at speeches rank, to weep at woes,
Or to turn white and swound at tragic shows:

'That not a heart which in his level came
Could scape the hail of his all-hurting aim,
Showing fair nature is both kind and tame;
And, veil'd in them, did win whom he would maim:
Against the thing he sought he would exclaim;
When he most burnt in heart-wisht luxury,
He preacht pure maid, and praised cold chastity.

'Thus merely with the garment of a Grace
The naked and concealed fiend he cover'd;
That th' unexperient gave the tempter place,
Which, like a cherubin, above them hover'd.
Who, young and simple, would not be so lover'd?
Ay me! I fell; and yet do question make
What I should do again for such a sake.

'O, that infected moisture of his eye,
O, that false fire which in his cheek so glow'd,
O, that forced thunder from his heart did fly,
O, that sad breath his spongy lungs bestow'd,
O, all that borrow'd motion seeming ow'd,
Would yet again betray the fore-betray'd,
And new pervert a reconciled maid!'

THE PASSIONATE PILGRIM

When my love swears that she is made of truth,
I do believe her, though I know she lies,
That she might think me some untutor'd youth,
Unskilful in the world's false forgeries.
Thus vainly thinking that she thinks me young,
Although I know my years be past the best,
I smiling credit her false-speaking tongue,
Outfacing faults in love with love's ill rest.
But wherefore says my love that she is young?
And wherefore say not I that I am old?
O, love's best habit is a soothing tongue,
And age, in love, loves not to have years told.
　　Therefore I'll lie with love, and love with me,
　　Since that our faults in love thus smother'd be.

Two loves I have, of comfort and despair,
That like two spirits do suggest me still;
My better angel is a man right fair,
My worser spirit a woman colour'd ill.
To win me soon to hell, my female evil
Tempteth my better angel from my side,
And would corrupt my saint to be a devil,
Wooing his purity with her fair pride.
And whether that my angel be turn'd fiend,
Suspect I may, yet not directly tell:
For being both to me, both to each friend,
I guess one angel in another's hell:
　　The truth I shall not know, but live in doubt,
　　Till my bad angel fire my good one out.

Did not the heavenly rhetoric of thine eye,
'Gainst whom the world could not hold argument,
Persuade my heart to this false perjury?
Vows for thee broke deserve not punishment.
A woman I forswore; but I will prove,
Thou being a goddess, I forswore not thee:
My vow was earthly, thou a heavenly love;
Thy grace being gain'd cures all disgrace in me.
My vow was breath, and breath a vapour is;
Then, thou fair sun, that on this earth doth shine,
Exhale this vapour vow; in thee it is:
If broken, then it is no fault of mine.
　　If by me broke, what fool is not so wise
　　To break an oath, to win a paradise?

Sweet Cytherea, sitting by a brook
With young Adonis, lovely, fresh and green,
Did court the lad with many a lovely look,
Such looks as none could look but beauty's queen.
She told him stories to delight his ear,
She show'd him favours to allure his eye; .
To win his heart, she toucht him here and there;
Touches so soft still conquer chastity.
But whether unripe years did want conceit,
Or he refused to take her figured proffer,
The tender nibbler would not touch the bait,
But smile and jest at every gentle offer:
    Then fell she on her back, fair queen, and toward:
    He rose and ran away; ah, fool too froward.

If love make me forsworn, how shall I swear to love?
O never faith could hold, if not to beauty vowed:
Though to myself forsworn, to thee I'll constant prove;
Those thoughts, to me like oaks, to thee like osiers bowed
Study his bias leaves, and makes his book thine eyes,
Where all those pleasures live that art can comprehend.
If knowledge be the mark, to know thee shall suffice;
Well learned is that tongue that well can thee commend:
All ignorant that soul that sees thee without wonder;
Which is to me some praise, that thy parts admire:
Thine eye Jove's lightning seems, thy voice his dreadful thunder,
Which, not to anger bent, is music and sweet fire.
    Celestial as thou art, O do not love that wrong,
    To sing heaven's praise with such an earthly tongue.

Scarce had the sun dried up the dewy morn,
And scarce the herd gone to the hedge for shade,
When Cytherea, all in love forlorn,
A longing tarriance for Adonis made
Under an osier growing by a brook,
A brook where Adon used to cool his spleen:
Hot was the day; she hotter that did look
For his approach, that often there had been.
Anon he comes, and throws his mantle by,
And stood stark naked on the brook's green brim:
The sun lookt on the world with glorious eye,
Yet not so wistly as this queen on him.
    He, spying her, bounced in, whereas he stood:
    'O Jove,' quoth she, 'why was not I a flood!'

Fair is my love, but not so fair as fickle,
Mild as a dove, but neither true nor trusty,
Brighter than glass and yet, as glass is, brittle,
Softer than wax and yet as iron rusty.
    A lily pale, with damask dye to grace her,
    None fairer, nor none falser to deface her.

Her lips to mine how often hath she joined,
Between each kiss her oaths of true love swearing!
How many tales to please me hath she coined,
Dreading my love, the loss whereof still fearing!
    Yet in the midst of all her pure protestings,
    Her faith, her oaths, her tears, and all were jestings.

She burnt with love, as straw with fire flameth;
She burnt out love, as soon as straw out-burneth;
She framed the love, and yet she foil'd the framing;
She bade love last, and yet she fell a-turning.
    Was this a lover, or a lecher whether?
    Bad in the best, though excellent in neither.

If music and sweet poetry agree,
As they must needs, the sister and the brother,
Then must the love be great 'twixt thee and me,
Because thou lovest the one and I the other.
Dowland to thee is dear, whose heavenly touch
Upon the lute doth ravish human sense;
Spenser to me, whose deep conceit is such
As passing all conceit needs no defence.
Thou lovest to hear the sweet melodious sound
That Phoebus' lute, the queen of music, makes;
And I in deep delight am chiefly drown'd
Whenas himself to singing he betakes.
    One god is god of both, as poets feign;
    One knight loves both, and both in thee remain.

Fair was the morn when the fair queen of love,
Paler for sorrow than her milk-white dove,
For Adon's sake, a youngster proud and wild;
Her stand she takes upon a steep-up hill:
Anon Adonis comes with horn and hounds;
She, silly queen, with more than love's good will,
Forbade the boy he should not pass those grounds:
'Once,' quoth she, 'did I see a fair sweet youth
Here in these brakes deep-wounded with a boar,
Deep in the thigh, a spectacle of ruth!
See, in my thigh,' quoth she, 'here was the sore.'
    She showed hers: he saw more wounds than one,
    And blushing fled, and left her all alone.

Sweet rose, fair flower, untimely pluckt, soon vaded,
Pluckt in the bud and vaded in the spring!
Bright orient pearl, alack, too timely shaded!
Fair creature, kill'd too soon by death's sharp sting!
 Like a green plum that hangs upon a tree,
 And falls through wind before the fall should be.

I weep for thee and yet no cause I have;
For why thou left'st me nothing in thy will:
And yet thou left'st me more than I did crave;
For why I craved nothing of thee still:
 O yes, dear friend, I pardon crave of thee,
 Thy discontent thou didst bequeath to me.

Venus, with young Adonis sitting by her
Under a myrtle shade, began to woo him:
She told the youngling how god Mars did try her,
And as he fell to her, so fell she to him.
'Even thus,' quoth she, 'the warlike god embraced me,'
And then she clipt Adonis in her arms;
'Even thus,' quoth she, 'the warlike god unlaced me,'
As if the boy should use like loving charms;
'Even thus,' quoth she, 'he seized on my lips,'
And with her lips on his did act the seizure:
And as she fetched breath, away he skips,
And would not take her meaning nor her pleasure.
 Ah, that I had my lady at this bay.
 To kiss and clip me till I run away!

Crabbed age and youth cannot live together:
Youth is full of pleasance, age is full of care;
Youth like summer morn, age like winter weather;
Youth like summer brave, age like winter bare.
Youth is full of sport, age's breath is short;
Youth is nimble, age is lame;
Youth is hot and bold, age is weak and cold;
Youth is wild, and age is tame.
Age, I do abhor thee; youth, I do adore thee;
O, my love, my love is young!
 Age, I do defy thee: O, sweet shepherd, hie thee,
 For methinks thou stay'st too long.

Beauty is but a vain and doubtful good;
A shining gloss that vadeth suddenly;
A flower that dies when first it gins to bud;
A brittle glass that's broken presently:
 A doubtful good, a gloss, a glass, a flower,
 Lost, vaded, broken, dead within an hour.

And as goods lost are seld or never found,
As vaded gloss no rubbing will refresh,
As flowers dead lie wither'd on the ground,
As broken glass no cement can redress,
    So beauty blemisht once for ever lost,
    In spite of physic, painting, pain and cost.

Good night, good rest. Ah, neither be my share:
She bade good night that kept my rest away;
And daft me to a cabin hang'd with care,
To descant on the doubts of my decay.
    'Farewell,' quoth she, 'and come again to-morrow:'
    Fare well I could not, for I supt with sorrow.

Yet at my parting sweetly did she smile,
In scorn or friendship, nill I conster whether:
'T may be, she joy'd to jest at my exile,
'T may be, again to make me wander thither:
    'Wander,' a word for shadows like myself,
    As take the pain, but cannot pluck the pelf.

Lord, how mine eyes throw gazes to the east!
My heart doth charge the watch; the morning rise
Doth cite each moving sense from idle rest.
Not daring trust the office of mine eyes,
    While Philomela sits and sings, I sit and mark,
    And wish her lays were tuned like the lark;

For she doth welcome daylight with her ditty,
And drives away dark dreaming night:
The night so packt, I post unto my pretty;
Heart hath his hope and eyes their wished sight;
    Sorrow changed to solace and solace mixt with sorrow;
    For why she sigh'd, and bade me come to-morrow.

Were I with her, the night would post too soon;
But now are minutes added to the hours;
To spite me now, each minute seems a moon;
Yet not for me, shine sun to succour flowers!
    Pack night, peep day; good day, of night now borrow:
    Short, night, to-night, and length thyself tomorrow.

Question: Is *The Passionate Pilgrim* a collection of sonnets/verses written by a poet who could not sleep because of erotic dreams?
Answer: Who knows?

SELECTED POEMS

It was a lording's daughter, the fairest one of three,
That liked of her master as well as well might be,
Till looking on an Englishman, the fair'st that eye could see,
　　Her fancy fell a-turning.

Long was the combat doubtful that love with love did fight,
To leave the master loveless, or kill the gallant knight:
To put in practice either, alas, it was a spite
　　Unto the silly damsel!

But one must be refused; more mickle was the pain
That nothing could be used to turn them both to gain,
For of the two the trusty knight was wounded with disdain:
　　Alas, she could not help it!

Thus art with arms contending was victor of the day,
Which by a gift of learning did bear the maid away:
Then, lullaby, the learned man hath got the lady gay;
　　For now my song is ended.

On a day, alack the day!
Love, whose month was ever May,
Spied a blossom passing fair,
Playing in the wanton air:
Through the velvet leaves the wind
All unseen gan passage find;
That the lover, sick to death,
Wisht himself the heaven's breath,
'Air,' quoth he, 'thy cheeks may blow;
Air, would I might triumph so!
But, alas! my hand hath sworn
Ne'er to pluck thee from thy thorn:
Vow, alack! for youth unmeet:
Youth, so apt to pluck a sweet.
Thou for whom Jove would swear
Juno but an Ethiope were;
And deny himself for Jove,
Turning mortal for thy love.'

LIVE WITH ME AND BE MY LOVE

Live with me, and be my love,
And we will all the pleasures prove
That hills and valleys, dales and fields,
And all the craggy mountains yields.

There will we sit upon the rocks,
And see the shepherds feed their flocks,
By shallow rivers, by whose falls
Melodious birds sing madrigals.

There will I make thee a bed of roses,
With a thousand fragrant posies,
A cap of flowers, and a kirtle
Embroider'd all with leaves of myrtle.

A belt of straw and ivy buds,
With coral clasps and amber studs;
And if these pleasures may thee move,
Then live with me and be my love.

Love's Answer

If that the world and love were young,
And truth in every shepherd's tongue,
These pretty pleasures might me move
To live with thee and be thy love.

Did Shakespeare write this poem?

Shakespeare was a natural genius. He was writing plays at the rate of two a year. He was also a businessman, perhaps inheriting that instinct from his father.

He aspired to be a gentleman, and even made a small investment in malt, which was then Stratford's principal industry.

Was it possible for him to write this poem? His sonnets established him during his lifetime as a poetic genius, and *'Live With Me and Be My Love'* is also attributed to him.

When you read his plays you can imagine this poem included in one of them. Perhaps he wrote it and decided, at the last moment, to leave it out.

He was a good scriptwriter. Will we ever know?

AS IT FELL UPON A DAY

As it fell upon a day
In the merry month of May,
Sitting in a pleasant shade
Which a grove of myrtles made,
Beasts did leap and birds did sing,
Trees did grow and plants did spring;
Every thing did banish moan,
Save the nightingale alone:
She, poor bird, as all forlorn,
Lean'd her breast up-till a thorn,
And there sung the dolefull'st ditty,
That to hear it was great pity:
'Fie, fie, fie,' now would she cry;
'Tereu, Tereu!' by and by;
That to hear her so complain,
Scarce I could from tears refrain;
For her griefs so lively shown
Made me think upon mine own.
Ah, thought I, thou mourn'st in vain!
None takes pity on thy pain:
Senseless trees they cannot hear thee;
Ruthless beasts they will not cheer thee:
King Pandion he is dead;
All thy friends are lapt in lead;
All thy fellow birds do sing,
Careless of thy sorrowing.
Even so, poor bird, like thee,
None alive will pity me.
Whilst as fickle Fortune smiled,
Thou and I were both beguiled.
Every one that flatters thee
Is no friend in misery.
Words are easy, like the wind;
Faithful friends are hard to find:
Every man will be thy friend
Whilst thou hast wherewith to spend;
But if store of crowns be scant,
No man will supply thy want.
If that one be prodigal,
Bountiful they will him call,

And with such-like flattering,
'Pity but he were a king;'
If he be addict to vice,
Quickly him they will entice;
If to women he be bent,
They have at commandement:
But if Fortune once do frown,
Then farewell his great renown;
They that fawn'd on him before
Use his company no more.
He that is thy friend indeed,
He will help thee in thy need:
If thou sorrow, he will weep;
If thou wake, he cannot sleep;
Thus of every grief in heart
He with thee doth bear a part.
These are certain signs to know
Faithful friend from flattering foe.

SHAKESPEARE ON THE SCREEN

Will lived near Bishopsgate when he wrote his greatest plays. They were written during the first decade of his company's occupation of the Globe. Then he moved to Southwark, although maintaining his financial interests in Stratford-upon-Avon.

His contemporaries honoured him as a poet and as a playwright, so it is probable that the poems ascribed to him were indeed composed by him. Playwrights are rarely poets. That is what distinguished Shakespeare from the rest.

His plays, because they gave actors an opportunity for histrionic expression, appealed to film-makers from the earliest days of commercial theatre. The first 'talkie' was *The Taming of the Shrew* with Douglas Fairbanks and Mary Pickford in 1929. In 1936 Max Reinhardt, who had staged *Midsummer Night's Dream* many times in Europe and America, directed a Hollywood film version with James Cagney as 'Bottom' and Mickey Rooney as 'Puck'.

How 'Will' would have chuckled as he banked the dollars!

Lawrence Olivier, as actor and director, made popular movies of *Henry V, Hamlet* and *Richard III*, and Orson Welles had a go with *Macbeth* and *Othello*.

Other productions have included Franco Zeffirelli's *'The Taming of the Shrew'* (1966), and *Romeo and Juliet* (1968). Roman Polanski's *Macbeth* (1971) was also very popular. *Hamlet* (1964) and *King Lear* (1971) by the Russian director Grigori Kozintsev, and Japanese versions of the Macbeth and Lear stories by Akira Kuroswawa have been widely acclaimed.

THE PHOENIX AND TURTLE

Let the bird of loudest lay,
On the sole Arabian tree,
Herald sad and trumpet be,
To whose sound chaste wings obey.

But thou shrieking harbinger,
Foul precurrer of the fiend,
Augur of the fever's end,
To this troop come thou not near!

From this session interdict
Every fowl of tyrant wing,
Save the eagle, feather'd king:
Keep the obsequy so strict.

Let the priest in surplice white,
That defunctive music can,
Be the death-divining swan,
Lest the requiem lack his right.

And thou treble-dated crow,
That thy sable gender makest
With the breath thou givest and takest.
'Mongst our mourners shalt thou go.

Here the anthem doth commence:
Love and constancy is dead;
Phoenix and the turtle fled
In a mutual name from hence.

So they loved, as love in twain
Had the essence but in one;
Two distincts, division none:
Number there in love was slain.

Hearts remote, yet not asunder;
Distance, and no space was seen
'Twixt the turtle and his queen:
But in them it were a wonder.

So between them love did shine,
That the turtle saw his right
Flaming in the Phoenix' sight;
Either was the other's mine.

Property was thus appalled,
That the self was not the same;
Single nature's double name
Neither two nor one was called.

Reason, in itself confounded,
Saw division grow together,
To themselves yet either neither,
Simple were so well compounded,

That it cried, How true a twain
Seemeth this concordant one!
Love hath reason, reason none,
If what parts can so remain.

Whereupon it made this threne
To the Phoenix and the dove,
Co-supremes and stars of love,
As chorus to their tragic scene.

Threnos

Beauty, truth, and rarity,
Grace in all simplicity,
Here enclosed in cinders lie.

Death is now the Phoenix' nest;
And the turtle's loyal breast
To eternity doth rest,

Leaving no posterity:
'Twas not their infirmity,
It was married chastity.

Truth may seem, but cannot be;
Beauty brag, but 'tis not she;
Truth and beauty buried be.

To this urn let those repair
That are either true or fair;
For these dead birds sigh a prayer.

This poem appeared in Robert Chester's 'Love's Martyr' in 1601

HE'S MORE THAN GLOBAL

He's universal.

That means that when humankind has colonised itself on the Moon or Mars, or wherever the environment is suitable for the continuation of human life, Shakespeare will be there to enthral them.

At present his plays, in book form, on screen and on television, are only available in Finland, Chile, Ethiopia, Tonga, North Korea, the United States, Canada, Brazil, Russia, South Africa, Australia, New Zealand and, of course, in the British Isles.

In the United Kingdom alone there are approximately 3,000 performances of his plays every year. That includes professional productions, amateur music and drama group productions and schools.

Global performances total approximately 50,000 every year.

Of his 37 plays the most popular are *A Midsummer Night's Dream* (remember Bottom?), *As You Like It* (very romantic), *The Merchant of Venice* (including Portia and Shylock), *Twelfth Night* (Malvolio's amusing), *Hamlet* (plenty of mayhem), *Macbeth* (more mayhem), *Romeo and Juliet* (love **and** mayhem), *Much Ado About Nothing* (a popular comedy) and *Othello* (you devil, Iago!).

For all this we have to thank two of Shakespeare's fellow-actors: John Heminges and Henry Condell. They collected his plays after his death on St. George's Day in 1623. It was a vast undertaking, without which 20 of his plays might have been lost forever.

The folio they were able to publish was re-published in 1632, 1664 and 1685, and the first scholarly edition followed in 1709, edited by the playwright Nicholas Rowe.

Rowe (1674-1718) was a playwright, poet and editor. He trained for the law, and afterwards served as Secretary of State for Scotland 1709-11, and was Poet Laureate from 1715 until his death.

His competent handling of blank verse was extravagantly admired by his contemporaries and even praised by Dr. Johnson!

He was able to compare copies of manuscripts, make emendations where he felt them necessary, and supply logical act and scene divisions.

A Shakespeare play performed on stage, screen or television, is not quite as Shakespeare's actors played it. Nor is the stage setting the same. But in every case Shakespeare's creative genius shines through.

It is unlikely to be repeated.